"Novelists never thrive in colonies.
Ants do. What budding novelists
Need is the privilege of wrestling
With their problems in solitude –
And now and then a piece of red meat."

With apologies to
Henry Miller

... other works by R. Karl Largent

Fiction

Black Death
The Prometheus Project
Ancients
Pagoda
The Witch of Sixkill
The Pond
Amityville – The Nightmare Continues
The Lake
Red Tide
Red Ice
Red Skies
Red Sand
Red Wind
The Sea
The Jakarta Plot (Scheduled for 1999 release)
The Gehenna Effect (Scheduled for 2000 release)

Nonfiction

A Pony is Not a Baby Horse
Getting Started – Handbook for the Beginning Novelist
Getting Published – How the Pros Do It
                (co – authored with Matthew V. Clemens)
Write Tight and Right – Effective Business Writing
                (co – authored with Dr. Earl Conn)
Get a Job – A Guide for Rotten Resume Writers

HOW TO WRITE AND

SELL YOUR NOVEL

... HANDBOOK FOR THE

BEGINNING NOVELIST

By

R. KARL LARGENT

Robin Vincent PUBLISHING

**How To Write and Sell Your Novel ... Handbook For the
Beginning Novelist**
R. Karl Largent

Robin Vincent Publishing LLC
2829 Grand Avenue
Davenport, IA 52803
(319) 323-6014

First Printing: 1999

Library of Congress Catalog Number: 99-64888

ISBN: 0–9645606–2-3

ACKNOWLEDGEMENTS

To Stephanie Keenan and Pam Clemens:
Many, many, many thanks.

About the Author

R. Karl Largent, a.k.a. Robin Karl or Simon Lawrence, is an author, lecturer, and columnist. Before launching his writing and teaching career, he spent thirty years in industry, the last seventeen as VP of Marketing for an Indiana-based Fortune 500 multinational.

Largent brings an intriguing and varied collection of life experiences to his present career. A former horse show judge and trainer of youth horses, he competed in SCCA road racing events, flew as a Weather Officer in the USAF, and served with the U.S. Weather Bureau. He holds degrees from Saint Francis College and Indiana University and is a recipient of the Dorothy Hamilton Award for lifetime achievement. He and his wife, Wilma, live on a lake in northern Indiana.

A note from the author …

This whole project began with a phone call. Some dear soul (whose name, regrettably, I have long since forgotten) at Fort Wayne's regional Indiana University campus called me questioning whether I would be interested in teaching a fiction writing class. It escapes me why I said yes. I had no teaching experience, no syllabus, and no idea how to prepare for such a venture. On the other hand, I had written and sold three novels (plus two others that have never seen the light of day) and I had made every mistake imaginable in crafting these early works.

So why a "How to book?"

No one needs to tell you there are dozens of books on the market on how to write a novel. Maybe you have waded through one or two of them. Some of these efforts are painfully uninformative (totally forgetting their purpose) and others drag the aspiring writer through other authors' own cathartic experiences as they worked their way through their early novels.

Not this "How to book."

To develop my seminar on writing, I took my notes, scratches, mental meanderings, and anything else I thought I had learned in writing those early novels to Professor Steve Hollander, IU's writing guru at IPFW, and he helped me massage it into a five-hour seminar. In the years since, I have presented my seminar, *The Mechanics of Writing a Novel* (sometimes called *How to Write and Sell Your Novel*), to more than two thousand aspiring novelists (I quit counting at 2,113 seminar attendees more than a few years ago).

Needless to say, that writing seminar proved to be successful. Over the years, it has been presented at colleges and universities throughout Indiana, Michigan and Illinois. I have also had the good fortune to present some or all of the material in this book to such prestigious writing organizations as Mystery Writers of America, Romance Writers of America, and many, many other writing groups. In addition, the material has been presented at writers conferences in seven states.

So why is this "How to book" different?

It is a no-nonsense, practical, tool kit for the aspiring novelist. It tells you what works and what doesn't. It points out the kinds of writing sins that result in rejection slips. It tells you how to rewrite and polish, how to put together a solid commercial plot (one that sells), plus it delves into the world of constructing believable characters and writing crisp dialogue. It even gets into the subject of the all important submission package (marketing your novel) – and coping with the (gulp!) world of editors and literary agents.

Some of you may have purchased my first effort at a book of this nature titled, *Getting Started*, published in 1992. Even so, I believe you'll find this book to be more informative and even more helpful than the first. This book includes additional material on dialogue, on putting together a working outline, writing an extended synopsis (many editors and agents will require one when you are ready to market your manuscript), and much, much more. This latest effort also includes actual examples of outlines, manuscript synopsis, letters to agents, and some of the other documents that seem to both daunt and mystify new writers.

As you work your way through the following pages, you'll get a real nuts and bolts approach to writing a novel. I have made a concerted effort to eliminate the esoteric, the obtuse, the vague, the arcane, and the enigmatic. The focus is not on what you write but how to avoid many of the pitfalls that will, in the majority of cases, kill your chances of getting your work published regardless of the genre.

As always, a work of this nature gets a great deal of nurturing. Continued thanks to James V. Smith Jr., editor and publisher of my first effort at writing a handbook. Without his assistance, advice, and encouragement the first time around, this 1999 version of my book for aspiring novelists may very well have never have seen the light of day. To people like John Littell and Clive Cussler, Rod Serling and John D. MacDonald, and others; many, many thanks.

So much for that. I'll dally no longer, I know you are eager to get started.

So, let's do it.

Contents

REALITY CHECK

A young man attending one of my writing classes, when asked what he hoped to gain from the class, replied that he had just been laid off from his job and thought "he'd knock off a couple of novels, make a few bucks, and then go looking for another job."

His fellow seminar attendees were aghast. Most of us approach this task fully aware it just doesn't work that way. Writing a novel requires perseverance, commitment, and sweat. Writing a novel can be a long, lonely, often frustrating, and tedious journey with no guarantee of reward, either psychic or financial, at the end of your odyssey. But, if you are successful, the rewards are immeasurable.

Having said that, if you're with me, let's go about the business of getting started.

FIRST THINGS FIRST ...

How to Write and Sell Your Novel is designed to help you get started on and work your way through your first novel with a minimum of grief. If you have already attended one of my seminars, much of what you find in this book will remind, help you recall, and reinforce some of the material we covered that day. If not, no sweat; this book is designed to stand by itself. In fact, you'll discover many things in this updated and revised version of my earlier effort that in all likelihood weren't covered during that six and one-half hour seminar.

I wrote *How to Write and Sell Your Novel* because I was unable to find a nuts and bolts book about writing a novel when I started. It's a fact – if you're a novice, this book will help you. It is my belief *How to Write and Sell Your Novel* will not only help you avoid many of the traps I fell into when I started, but hopefully it will also encourage and inspire you. I truly believe, if you really want to, are willing to work hard, and have a good enough story to tell:

You can write a novel.

OKAY, LET'S GET STARTED...

USING THIS BOOK —
LET'S START WITH DIFFERENT WAYS YOU CAN
USE THIS BOOK.
YOU CAN:

1.   Read it.

2.   Take notes.

3.   Underline.

4.   Jot down stuff in the margins.

5.   Wade through it chapter by chapter.

6.   Do <u>Calisthenics</u> when the book suggests.

7.   Keep a journal, particularly in those sections where you feel you need lots of help.

8.   Look for and jot down tips, neat tricks, traps to avoid, and plain old inspiration.

9.   Pay attention to the <u>Pitfalls</u>.

10.   Refer back to the <u>Short</u> <u>Lists</u> when you're stuck.

DEFINITION: COMMERCIAL NOVEL:

Let me put it this way: A commercial novel is one that sells.

THE UP SIDE ... GOOD STUFF
MONETARY REWARD

Commercial fiction usually earns the author an advance against royalties. If it sells enough copies to offset the advance, it may also generate future royalties. Neat, huh? I'd be willing to bet this is exactly what you had in mind when you bought this book. Right?

PSYCHIC REWARD

Write a good-enough novel and you'll get an even niftier reward, you'll see it on the bookshelves each time you walk into a bookstore. Believe me, *psychic reward* is almost as good as money.

THE DOWN SIDE...THE BAD STUFF
IT MAY NOT SELL

After a faltering start some twenty years earlier, I wrote two novels in the early Eighties. Neither saw the light of day. No one has ever read them. Why? Well, the fact of the matter is they weren't very well done.

BUT...

In the process of churning out those two works, I proved one thing to myself. I proved I could do it; I could and did write a novel. I wrote four hundred pages for each one and they had a beginning, a middle, and an end. Then, when I wrote my third novel, I applied what I had learned and sold it.

YOUR NOVEL ISN'T A HOWLING FINANCIAL SUCCESS

Keep in mind, even if your first novel isn't the howling financial success you hoped it would be (and it probably won't be – because those readers out there don't know the quality of your work or your name yet), you've taken the first, giant step toward a career in writing.

BUT...

One more thing to think about: You're no longer just another writer, you're an *author*. What's the difference? Well, as Matthew V. Clemens puts it, "Writers write, *authors* get published." The bottom line to all of this is you can't believe how much easier it is to sell your next novel after you've sold that first one.

WAYS OF PLYING YOUR CRAFT

If you were to listen to or read what ten different successful novelists had to say about their craft, I feel certain you would hear each of them emphasize different aspects of their expertise:

1.   Clive Cussler (*Raise the Titanic*) takes as long to research his novels as he does to write them.

2.   Other authors I know spend five times as much time editing and revising as they do constructing their original draft.

3.   Still others, Mickey Spillane for example, leave editing and revision to their editors. (Don't try this unless you've produced the kind of publishing numbers Mr. Spillane has.)

The point is that different authors have different ways of plying their craft, but they all have certain mechanical things they do in order to write a novel. This book will show you how to use those tools.

1.   In the pages that follow I will suggest that you engage in some simple writing drills. These <u>Calisthenics</u> will help you write tighter (a necessity in today's commercial fiction).

2.   I will also show you how to avoid many of the <u>Pitfalls</u> that other writers have fallen into on their attempts to write a novel.

3.   I will help you construct a "get action" query letter and a synopsis; both of which are required when you are ready to submit your work to a publisher or agent.

IT'S TRUE — THIS BOOK IS FOR BEGINNERS...

I've had published authors tell me they learned something from it as well. Nevertheless, this book was written for the beginner. It will give you the over-the-shoulder guidance the novice wants and often needs.

ALONG THE WAY YOU'LL SEE HOW TO:
1.   Construct believable characters.
2.   Write clean, crisp, believable dialogue.
3.   Develop your style.
4.   Design your plot and elude plot shortcomings.
5.   Deal with problems you've never thought about.

Remember this:

This is a true nuts and bolts kind of book. The whole purpose is to help you learn how to go about constructing good commercial fiction. Ready?

LET'S GET STARTED...

5

FIRST THINGS FIRST –
THE SHORT LIST

1. A **Commercial Novel** is one that sells.

2. The **Up Side** is writing to sell leads to monetary and psychic rewards.

3. The **Down Side** is your writing may not sell or it may not be a success.

4. Different authors have different ways of plying their craft, **but they all have certain mechanical things they do in order to write a novel.**

2

LET'S DO IT ...

FIRST: *NO EXCUSES* — If you really want to write a novel, there is no reason for not starting <u>now</u>. Know the difference between a reason and an excuse. Reasons are valid. Excuses like these are not:

1. I was a C student in college composition class.
2. I never understood dangling participles or antecedent whatevers.
3. And the big one:
   I DON'T HAVE TIME.

SECOND: YOU CAN'T EXPECT TO FIND TIME ... YOU MUST *MAKE TIME*.

1. Get up off the couch, turn off the TV, and get going.
2. Folks with backbreaking schedules like doctors, young mothers with toddlers, and business executives make time.
3. Schedule it into your daily agenda.

THIRD: YOU MUST BE WILLING TO PROVIDE 90% PERSPIRATION, then in this book I'll help you discover the other 10% — inspiration and creativity.

MY EXPERIENCE: Pre author days ...

I worked a sometimes sixty-hour week back in my pre-author days. I traveled all over the country. I wrote in airports, on flights, in motels at night, on weekends, during lunch hours, on holidays, and vacations. (No lap top, just pen and paper. I transcribed my scribbling to a word processor when I got home.) Two of the three books written under those conditions were published.

PITFALL

If you're willing to lean on the excuse, "I just don't have time," you very likely haven't yet developed that old fire in the belly that is required to write a novel.

TO BECOME A NOVELIST...

1. Writing has to be your <u>fix</u>.
2. Telling a good story has to be your <u>obsession</u>.
3. Writing a novel cannot be a <u>want to</u>. It cannot be a <u>plan to</u>.
4. Nor can it be an <u>I'd like to</u> thing.
5. Not even a fundamental love of writing will do, but it is a good start.
6. Nothing short of <u>*obsessive, compulsive behavior*</u> supported by good writing habits will get the job done.
7. Your desire to become a novelist has to be strong enough to keep you going when your butt is tired, your head aches, the right words aren't coming to you and everyone else is camped out at the pool or curled up taking naps. My agent and my editor work hard every day; they expect no less of me.

PITFALL
Don't be discouraged by false starts.
Even if you work smart and hard, you
have to expect false starts and setbacks.

MY EXPERIENCE: Never give up ...

Up until I began writing again in the early Eighties, my own efforts at writing a novel amounted to little more than faltering starts and a whole lot of frustration. I was probably in the same position many of you find yourself in today: I wanted to write, but I did not know how to get started and I had no idea how to sustain the effort after I did get started.

Let me catapult you back several years. Shortly after the assassination of President Kennedy, I took a business trip to Salt Lake City. I learned that Brigham Young's forward-thinking and superb planning made a significant contribution to the opening up of the American West.

Idea! Suppose someone had assassinated Brigham Young before he had the opportunity to implement his agenda for the city? How would the West have been different?

Well, to make an already long story even longer, I came home, put the idea to paper and, 355 pages later, fired it off to an agent in New York. Guess what happened?

The book was rejected.

But here's the rub. The agent I submitted the book to actually went to the trouble of writing me a seven-page letter critiquing the manuscript. He told me what I needed to do to make the manuscript publishable. Cool, huh? Might have been cool but I was so naïve I didn't recognize the value of professional criticism. (I was reading between the lines: He didn't like it.) Instead of incorporating the suggested changes, I

9

put the manuscript away and didn't try to write again for twenty years.

Dumb! Dumb! Dumb! Don't make the same mistake I did. Don't let a setback (read that frustration, ignorance, or pride) get in the way of your reaching your goal of becoming published. If you learn nothing else from this book, learn that you should never give up.

How it all got started again:

Twenty years later, while returning from a business trip, a colleague asked me what my personal goals were.

I thought for a moment and finally admitted, "Someday I want to write a novel."

"What's holding you back?" my colleague probed.

"I just don't have the time," I said.

Then my friend said something that I realize now, in retrospect, altered my life. *"You could get started."*

There is no defense against truth.

Remember these four words the next time you decide you don't have time to write your novel.

I took the advice, started keeping a log of how often I had the opportunity to write, and within one month had worked my way up to twenty hours a week. By the end of the fourth month I was writing thirty hours a week.

Think about it. How long do you get for lunch? Cut the time in half and use the rest to write. Instead of spending two hours in front of the tube each evening, cut your viewing time in half. Are you spending a couple of hours a day on a commuter train? Are you dozing off in your favorite chair after dinner? There is a lot of time out there – all you have to do is use it.

Now that you've thought about it, what's your reason? Or is it just an excuse? If it is an excuse, remember the four most important words a would-be author can hear:

YOU COULD GET STARTED

So why am I telling you all of this? Because...

1.   For the simple reason that if your desire to write is strong, that alone should be sufficient to make you sit down to start writing.
2.   At this point, don't be concerned with your questions about whether or not you have the talent or ability.
3.   Don't be worried about the rules of grammar or the proper formatting of a manuscript.
4.   We're talking here about the first hurdle in any creative endeavor:
The 90 percent factor known as <u>perspiration</u> (read that, the effort) it takes.

We'll work on the other 10 percent, the inspiration and the creativity, in subsequent chapters.

LET'S DO IT—THE SHORT LIST

1.   **Make time** to write.

2.   Be **obsessive**.

3.   **Don't sweat** whether you're good enough with **grammar and formatting**.

PLANS ...

A PLACE TO WRITE

FIRST: It should be a permanent place. Avoid trying to write in a place where you waste half your time setting up your equipment and getting everything arranged so you can begin writing. This is precious writing time lost.

SECOND: It should have no distractions. Get away from the phone. Tell your family when you're in your writing area, everything - all people, phone calls, or any other interruptions are forbidden.

THIRD: Your place should be conducive to writing. Crank up your favorite CD if it helps you write. I like a tape with the sounds of thunderstorms or Classical music.

PITFALL

I might as well say this now. No one – your
mate, your children, not even your closest
friend will understand what you are doing
when you hole up to write. At first, they'll
think you're going through some life change
or trauma. Finally (the time required to do
so varies) they begin to accept it. Final acceptance
of the new you, the writer, comes when you
receive a check from your publisher. Hey, is there
anyone out there who doesn't understand or can't
relate to a check?

YOUR PLAN

FIRST: Now that you have a place to write, let's tackle
the second problem: Know what you're going to
write about. The moment you can answer that,
all kinds of questions begin to boil up.

Question One: What is a good plan?

No where is it written that you have to follow
any plan to the letter. But I can assure you that
most successful authors have a set way of
beginning their writing, close to what will
follow.

Question Two: Why do I need a plan?

The whole process of writing your novel
becomes immeasurably easier when you have a
plan in place.

PITFALL
There's a good chance you won't buy the fact that you need to follow a set plan until you've written yourself into a corner somewhere along the way to the climax of your novel.

A PLAN THAT WORKS

1.   **CRYSTALLIZE YOUR IDEA**

2.   **DEVELOP YOUR IDEA**

3.   **DO THE NECESSARY RESEARCH**

4.   **OUTLINE YOUR NOVEL**

5.   **WRITE THE FIRST DRAFT**

6.   **REWRITE, REVISE, AND POLISH**

1. CRYSTALLIZE YOUR IDEA

On the surface at least, it seems fairly obvious. But you would be surprised how many aspiring novelists don't have a clear idea of where they are headed. Many have some big climactic scene that they want to work up but how they plan to get there is cloudy at best.

CALISTHENICS

Take a moment here and write down your idea:
Key words, key scenes, even a character sketch
or two.

The above exercise will help you bring your idea
more into focus.

Now, ask yourself: Is your idea a good one?

PITFALL

Often, students in my seminars are reluctant to
discuss their ideas for fear someone will steal them.
This is not a valid concern. Others will tell me
they have several ideas. This means they haven't
given the subject enough thought yet. And, I can
always count on some students saying something
that sounds like, "I want to write a novel about
my Aunt Gloria's quilt," or "I want to write a novel
about my Uncle Ebenezer, he's so funny."

Hey, reality check. Aunt Gloria's quilt better
be haunted, or Uncle Ebenezer's one-liners
better be real knee slappers if they are going
to carry a whole novel. To put it another way,
can they carry a 70,000 to 100,000 word novel?

The idea for a novel must be a BIG STORY idea. Editors are looking for big stories that can sustain a reader's interest for 400 pages.

2. DEVELOP YOUR IDEA

POV

Okay, you've passed the first major hurdle. You have a big story idea and it's a good one. Now we start dealing with the nuts and bolts. Answer this one: <u>What will be your point of view?</u> *POV.*

<u>THIRD PERSON</u>
The third person narrative (advisable on most first novels) provides the most freedom. And let me add this: I believe individual style comes more into play when an author works in the third person POV. This narrative style allows your reader to be omniscient. In other words, by telling your story from the perspective of the narrator, readers can know more than the characters in your plot, even to the point of being forewarned about impending disasters. This way, the reader can anticipate the outcome before it happens. Rod Serling, the genius behind television's *The Twilight Zone* and *Night Gallery,* claims that readers love knowing more about a situation than the character knows. An author I know claims that the third person POV works best with romance, horror, science fiction, westerns, and adventure novels.

17

FIRST PERSON

If you are writing in the first person, your reader will view everything through your protagonist's eyes. That means your protagonist has to be in every scene and has to see or overhear everything that takes place in your novel. "I overheard," "I saw him kill her," "She was the most beautiful woman I've ever seen." If you wrote that last sentence in third-person, it would read something like, "Bob fell in love with her the first time he saw her."

In the first person POV, you have to find a way to tell the character, "For Pete's sake, don't go in there," because the reader has no way of knowing that the creature is hiding in there.

My author friend tells me that first person POV works best with psychodramas and reflective works where the focus is more on the characters than on the convoluted plot.

PITFALL

All POVs have limitations. This mean you have to think through some of the more convoluted scenes to see which POV will work best for your particular novel.

CALISTHENICS

Try writing a scene from the two different POVs and see which works best.

SETTING

Where does the story take place? Have you been there?
Can you describe it? What about the period in which your story
takes place? If your story is set in the past, that implies a lot of
research. A contemporary setting requires a thorough
knowledge and understanding of what's going on in the world
now. Setting your story in the future is really tough because
you have to project your reader into a believable world 10, 20,
50, or more years into the future.

CALISTHENICS
Create your setting.

NUMBER OF CHARACTERS

How many characters do you need?
At this point in the crystallization process of your novel,
you need to be thinking about how many characters will be
needed to tell your story. How many primary, secondary and
even tertiary characters will be required? If you're going to tell
some multi-generational tale of epic proportions, you're really
going to have to think through this aspect of your novel. Or are
you only going to have four characters? You'd better be sure
that's all you'll need.

CALISTHENICS
List your characters.

3. DO THE NECESSARY RESEARCH

How much research is essential? It varies. In my horror writing genre days, not all that much research was necessary. All I needed was a solid sense of time and space. Now that I'm writing techno-thrillers, my nose is always buried in some arms manual or performance report of weapons' systems. If the latter sounds daunting, I have a marvelous tip to pass along in Chapter Five.

4. OUTLINE YOUR NOVEL

Seldom does any part of my lecture on novel development draw more furrowed foreheads, wrinkled noses, and expressions of dismay than the mention of outlining.

For most folks, the word outline conjures up visions of classroom busy work where each point in a lecture or article is painstakingly enumerated and all the subpoints indented, as in:

I. Main Idea
   A. Point I.
      1. More malarkey.
      2. Still more.
         a. is for absurd.
         b. is for baloney.

Relax. That's not what I'm talking about. I'm talking about sitting down and determining where you are going to start and how you intend to end. A writer's outline is nothing more than a map (your own personal cartogram), a guide from your beginning through all those convoluted subplots in the middle, and, ultimately, the smashing end of your story.

Your outline may just be as simple as 1. First thing that happens. 2. Second thing that happens. 3. Etc.

Most of my outlines, when I'm developing my ideas, turn out to be a couple of pages long.

PITFALL

Finally, a note to the reluctant outliner who may have run across an article in one of the writer's magazines authored by someone the caliber of John Gunther or William Peter Blatty who claim never to outline. If you are already an author of that stroke and bore, you probably wouldn't be reading or needing this handbook.

Reinforcement time:

I was sitting at a sidewalk cafe recently with a group of authors. Among them was Kathy Hammer, a very funny lady and successful author that many have tabbed the successor to Erma Bombeck. She said, "Show me a manuscript that wanders all over the place and I'll show you a writer who didn't bother to outline."

CALISTHENICS

Write a brief outline of your novel.

5. WRITE THE FIRST DRAFT

Now, you're ready for the fun part. You know where you are going, how to get there, and how long it will take—roughly. All your tools are laid out in front of you. The plot is crystallized, developed, researched, and outlined. So, now's the time to begin that first draft.

I do it this way: I start on page one and hammer away. I work as fast as I can (I shoot for seven pages of raw manuscript a day) until I get to page 400.

Do not: Stop to correct spelling mistakes...
Worry about punctuation and grammar...
Correct typos...

In fact, I don't worry about anything except getting the first blush of the story down on the paper. Only then do I know if I have a story worth telling — a story that will keep the reader turning pages.

At this point I ask myself questions:

1.   Is the story all there?

2.   Did I leave anything out?

3.   What did I overlook?

4.   Are there holes in the plot?

5.   Did I introduce my sub-plots at the right point?

6.   Are my main characters sympathetic enough for the reader to like them?

7.   And, the most <u>important question</u> of all: Will the story I have told be compelling enough to make people want to read it?

PITFALL

Be critical. Don't ask your mother or your best friend to read it, or even take it to your local writer's group. It isn't done yet. You have to be discriminating and self-assured enough to know whether or not it does what you want it to do. If it doesn't, fix it. If it works, and you like what you see, go forward.

6. REWRITE, REVISE, AND POLISH

Fix all those typos, misspellings, and punctuation errors. Reshape sentences; turn and twist phrases; take out extra words; find better nouns; more active verbs; delete as many -ly words as you can; make that gem shine. This is where you become a real writer, a real storyteller. If you do a good enough job, you may become an *author.*

BIG DEAL

Tell me about your novel. But restrict yourself
to **250 keyboarded words** (one page, double-spaced). I have
had hundreds of aspiring novelists tell me it can't be done. Then
they learn they can do it. (It was a requirement in Rod Serling's
workshops.)

This drill alone will tell you more about what you need to work
on in your writing style than any drill I know of.

PITFALL

Something to think about: If you can't perform the
above drill, if you can't discipline yourself to write
250 words now, what's the point of starting a novel?

A CAVEAT:

There are a few more things a beginning novelist needs
to know. Most established authors will tell you that an idea is
seldom born ready to be exploded into a full-blown novel. A
certain amount of tinkering is required. Take your idea and turn
it inside out. Spin it 180 degrees. See how it might play from a
different perspective. Does the story work better if you make
your killer a woman instead of a man? Would London work
better as a setting than Toledo? What historical elements can
you weave into your plot for added impact? Will an additional
conflict (sub-plot) add depth to your story idea? What about

the weather? What about the age of your protagonist? Keep this in mind: It takes a big story to write a novel. A little time spent playing "**what if**" with your plot may make your story line even stronger. The stronger the plot, the more likely it is to sell.

Okay? You are determined, right? Then go to it.

PLANS — THE SHORT LIST

1. A Place to Write:
Make sure it's permanent, has no distractions, and is conducive to writing.

2. Your Plan:
Create a good, solid BIG STORY plan.

3. A Plan That Works:

a. *Crystallize* your idea and make sure it's based on a BIG STORY idea.

b. Then *develop your plan* by deciding on POV, the setting, and your number of characters.

c. Do the necessary *research* and prepare an *outline*.

d. Have fun writing your *first draft* and write straight through from beginning to end.

e. Lastly, make it shine by *rewriting*, *revising*, and *polishing*.

4. Play the "What if?" Game:
See if there is anything you might want to or need to change. Ask 'what if' you told your story from another POV or used different characters or other settings.

IDEAS ...

FIRST: **Be patient. It takes a while for some ideas to come together.**

SECOND: **On the other hand, some ideas develop more easily.**

THIRD: **You may already have your idea, so GO FOR IT.**

DEVELOPMENT OF IDEAS:

John Littell, the former guru of Dorchester Publishing and one of my early mentors, once said, "A story idea can take two minutes or two years to develop; sometimes longer."

My Experience: The slow one...
How *Black Death* Came to Life ...

My first published novel, *Black Death*, spent a long time in the crucible. In fact, I didn't even realize it was happening at first.

The elements of the story came to me in dribs and drabs. It all began when a psychic I knew told me about a barren spot high on a hill on an Indiana farm overlooking the Ohio River. Despite repeated plowing and planting, several generations of owners were unable even to get weeds to grow on that spot. The psychic told me how she had visited the farm the previous summer and, when she approached the spot, she was overcome with feelings of foreboding, fell to her knees, began trembling, and broke into sobs (Move over Alfred Hitchcock).

I later learned about a site in the same vicinity where stories had it 20 Indian women and children were butchered by white trappers and buried in shallow graves.

At this point, two fragments of something were floating around in my brain, but the story still wasn't there.

It began to crystallize, however, when I visited a Shaker village outside of Berea, Kentucky, sometime later.

What if, I asked myself, a man who had been exposed to the bubonic plague in France came to America illegally? What if he sought refuge (to get away from the authorities) in that village, fell in love with a young Shaker woman, and they were forced to leave the settlement when they decided to marry? Where did they settle? You guessed it: On that hill, (in my mind at least) a lush spot ideal for building a home and starting a family.

At this point the whole idea was pretty fragile. It needed much more than I had. I began to fill in the voids. The couple's children, all stillborn, were buried in shallow graves on that hillside. But here's my kicker: Those children were all carriers of the plague. See how this idea was starting to come together?

Finally, I found the missing piece. Up the road from

where we lived at the time was a chemical plant. One day there was a chemical spill and the stream behind our house became contaminated after a heavy rain. The contamination lasted only a few days, but there it was ... the *idea* was beginning to come together. I worked out a plot where a heavy and prolonged rain, washing over the shallow graves of the children infected by their father, a man carrying the bacteria of the plague that killed thousands in Europe, was now contaminating the water supply of a sleepy southern Indiana village. A disaster of unspeakable proportions was in the making. It could not only wipe out the town; it would eventually leach into the Ohio River and ... See what I mean about a big story?

Like John Littell said, it takes awhile for some ideas to come together. That was certainly the case with *Black Death*.

The Fast One...

On the other hand, some ideas develop more easily. *The Pond*, my sixth novel, written under the name Simon Lawrence, is a case in point.

When *The Pond* was conceived, I was standing on our patio with a long-time friend, discussing our community, a small city of 25,000 with a strong economic base, outstanding school system, active civic participation, and prominent architecture.

"It sure is a model city," my friend said. "How do they do it?"

"It's the city fathers," I laughed. "They don't let anything happen that might detract from this town's reputation."

"That still doesn't explain how they do it," my friend said.

After he left, I thought about his off-hand remark and began to wonder how five or six very powerful men in a community would go about making their town "the perfect place to live."

Within days I had created Clayborn, Alabama, the ideal community: No garbage, no sickness, no old people, and no problems; a town with a sound economic base because it has a fertilizer company that funds continual civic improvements. Crystallization time: Less than two weeks. In this case the idea was born full blown and so complete that it took me only three months to write the novel. To this day I'm still convinced it's the best sinister fiction novel I've ever authored.

PITFALL

I can almost guarantee that no matter how much planning you put into your first novel, how much revising and editing you do, or how hard you work to make certain that every word is right, you will someday look back at what you have written and see all kinds of things you could have done to improve it. It goes with the territory. Don't get discouraged, it's all part of becoming an author.

SMILE ON FORTUNE

Having said all that, a word of caution is in order. If you are one of those fortunate few who is struck with that absolutely dynamite story idea and it comes to you ready for the telling, don't tamper with it. Just write it. Do not change for the sake of change.

IDEAS – THE SHORT LIST

1. Understand that **ideas can come slow or quick**.

2. **Give your ideas time** to come together. Don't get discouraged.

3. Let the idea **crystallize**.

4. **Smile on fortune**.

RESEARCH ...

FIRST: Begin with sources you are familiar with: A local library or location, a neighborhood used book store.

SECOND: Get into the habit of carrying a camera.

THIRD: Simplify your task. Write what you know.

FOURTH: Use a tape recorder and video recorder to help you recall images and burn the information into your mind.

My Experience: The easy one ...

Some commercial fiction requires a great deal of research and some doesn't. *Black Death*, for example, required very little. I could even take it a step further and say some genres don't require as much research as others.

I knew my setting for *Black Death* cold because I lived less than 50 miles away from where the story takes place. I knew the social patterns of southern Indiana communities. I knew the climate too. That was important because weather plays a big part in spreading disease in the story.

About the only research I had to do consisted of learning more about the bubonic plague and shooting a few rolls of film in several areas of Rising Sun, Indiana. For the story purposes, I changed the name of Rising Sun to Half Moon.

Ta da (musical sound). End of research.

With the snapshots pinned to my bulletin board just above my computer, I started writing and never looked back.

A RECOMMENDATION
Get in the habit of carrying a camera.
Take pictures of people, places, and
things that might fit in your novel.

The hard one ...
This was not the case with *Red Tide*, my first techno-thriller. This is a work with a very convoluted plot, more characters than I had ever worked with, and lots of high-tech equipment. To compound matters, fully one-third of the book was set in Moscow. Small problem: I had never been to Moscow, so I had a formidable task on that score.

Before even attempting to outline my plot (I did have a very nebulous story idea), I digested tons of reading material about Russia and state-of-the-art military equipment.

I read:
1. *Russia* by Harrison Salisbury
2. *The Soviet Union* by Harry P. Swartz
3. *Soviet Military Power Update*, a Pentagon document
4. *Polar Star* and *Gorky Park* by Martin Cruz Smith
5. *Atlas of Soviet Affairs* by Robert Ringsbury
6. *Soviet Union* by Lydle Brinkle
7. *The Defense Game* by Richard Stubbing
8. *Inside Soviet Military Intelligence* by Victor Suvorov

In addition **to reading, annotating, and tape recording excerpts from these books:**
I watched hours of relevant PBS documentaries at the

library and went through stacks of *Navy Times*, manuals on naval equipment, and weapons assessments.

Preparation time for *Red Tide*: About <u>seven months</u>.

<u>**Finally**</u>...
Armed with Russian dictionaries and street maps of Moscow, I was ready to write.

<u>**More Troubles**</u>...
Even then I ran into snag after snag. It was tough keeping track of time when events happened simultaneously in Washington, Jamaica, and Russia. (Russia alone has nine different time zones.) Which brings me to another suggestion:

A RECOMMENDATION
Your first novel is tough enough without having to do research by the metric ton. Simplify your task. Write what you know. If you are familiar with your topic, you reduce the things you have to research.

<u>**Still No Excuses Allowed:**</u>
What's that you say? Nothing exciting has ever happened to you. Followed, of course, by the question: How am I going to make a novel out of that stuff? Ask Tom Clancy that question. He was an insurance salesman when he wrote *Hunt for Red October*. Submarines and weaponry were his hobbies.

Remember the chapter on excuses? Go back and read it again. What you don't know, you can research. Research, like outlining, is a vital part of getting ready to write.

35

SOME SOLID WAYS TO RESEARCH
1. YOUR LIBRARY

I have mentioned several research resources already. For a writer though, your library ranks right up there next to your word processor as your best friend. Get familiar with your library. Better yet, go buy your librarian a cup of coffee occasionally; discuss your project with her. Then you'll be in position to call her and ask for information.

Even if your local library is a small one, it offers inter-library loans. Resource material once available only to people in communities with large libraries is now available to us small-town folk.

2. LOCATION
Read or travel ...

Years ago there were only two ways to do research. You could either read about it or you traveled to the location to experience matters first-hand. As you well know, the former can get tedious, the latter can get expensive.

3. ANOTHER OPTION
Haul out your tape recorder ...

A couple of years ago I was asked to develop some story lines for a television series. Since two of the episodes revolved around old Sherlock Holmes adventures, I rented old British Sherlock Holmes films and recorded the sound track while I watched the movies. I picked up clues to how Holmes dressed, the ambiance of London, and a host of other things. Plus, those tape recordings proved to be invaluable for picking up speech characteristics of both Holmes and Watson. Imagine how it simplified writing the dialogue.

A RECOMMENDATION

When I watch a documentary or educational film, I turn on my tape recorder and record the soundtrack. Then, when I'm driving, I replay those tapes. The voice-over narration recalls all the images and burns the information into my mind. This tip alone can reduce your research time by 50 percent.

4. OTHER RESEARCH MATERIAL

Learn to haunt used bookstores and college bookstores. Out-of-date textbooks are cheap and think how professional you'll sound when your physician protagonist explains the bullet shattered "the greater trochanter of the femur." That sounds a great deal more savvy than writing, "the hip."

THE WRITER'S SURVIVAL KIT

A few simple tools can make any research project a whole lot easier.

1. A CAMERA:

In my writer's survival kit I have an inexpensive, loaded camera. I have taken pictures of wrecks, houses, old buildings, people, trees, creeks, bridges, animals, boats, cars - just about anything that looks like it might be good reference material. I don't worry about composition, picture quality, or color. All I want that picture to do is help me recall the mood. Most of the time I use black and white film. For some reason black and white film seems to capture mood better than color.

2. A TAPE RECORDER:

Another useful tool is a tape recorder and a handful of cassettes. Cheap ones work fine. I catch interesting items on the radio, my thoughts, an impression of a passing scene, or the sudden idea that occurs to me – maybe one that solves a particular plot problem I've been mulling over. I should also mention that books on tape give you a great opportunity to listen to how other authors handle certain plot situations. They may even help you with some style problems.

3. THE INTERNET

These days, most authors I know utilize the Internet. One author I know claims that he has cut his research time in half by simply using the Internet. If you do not have access to this marvelous research tool, find someone who is already smitten by the computer bug and learn what the Internet has to offer.

PITFALL

A word of advice, though. Don't waste time browsing; you are cutting into your writing time.

My Experience: **Guilty of sloppy research ...**

Several years ago, I received a two-page letter from a reader who delighted in telling me I was guilty of sloppy research. She informed me that Reeboks weren't even on the market when my story was supposed to have taken place.

Who knows this stuff anyway?

You don't have to check every little detail. But before you hang yourself on some technical or historical fact or figure, check it.

      Back to the Reeboks. It was a blunder on my part and someone caught it. Readers are critical. That was fifteen years ago and now I beam with pride when I see a Reebok ad because I had the foresight to introduce the shoes two years ahead of the manufacturer.

RESEARCH – THE SHORT LIST

1. Check out familiar sources**: the library, the Internet, or used book stores.**

2. **Carry a camera** and take pictures.

3. **Simplify your task**. Write what you know.

4. **Use audio and video recorders** to help you recall information.

5. **Watch documentaries** and **record the soundtrack.**

6. **Put together your writer's survival kit**: A camera, a tape recorder, access to the Internet.

7. **Be thorough** – avoid sloppy research.

6

OUTLINING ...

FIRST: Just tell your story... scribble.

SECOND: Find the holes & recognize problems in the plot, then play "what if?"

THIRD: Make sense of the mishmash – get organized.

FOURTH: Review what you've got so far, delete the garbage – run the paranoia drill.

FACT: *A BEGINNING NOVELIST NEEDS AN OUTLINE!*

REDUCING THE PAIN

At this point, a few pointers and suggestions can reduce the pain in the outlining process.

1.   When I say outline, I mean the process of capturing the high points of your story and putting them down on paper – hopefully, eventually in chronological order.

2.   Tell your story just as you would tell a friend about the movie you saw the previous evening,

        from beginning to end.

3.   Trust me, a good outline will make the whole process of writing a novel a whole lot easier. Why would you want to make it any tougher?

      A.   I know authors who work from computerized outlines.

      B.   I know others who create a handwritten or typed "story board" for each chapter. In the last chapter of this book, I have included a copy of one of my outlines.

CALISTHENICS

When you finish this chapter on outlines I suggest you thumb back to that example and read it. It should, as an old business colleague of mine used to say, "diffuse the specter of a task far less daunting than it sounds."

MY WAY: FIRST, I SCRIBBLE

1.   I grab a tablet of paper and start scribbling all the events that I want to occur during the course of my novel.

2.   I spell out the problems and my proposed solutions.

3.   I rough out major scenes and the major conflicts I've thought out.

4.   Often, I make note of things I know won't work. Why? Well, because I have a poor memory, and I don't want to have to rethink these plot points over again at a later date. (Oh yeah, that's why I didn't have Elmer thrown

from a horse. I said earlier he hates horses. So why would he be riding one?)

SECOND, I RECOGNIZE PROBLEMS IN THE PLOT AND...

1. Several pages into this scribbling process, I usually begin to recognize some of the holes in my plot. For example, a particular sequence of events won't work if I place my protagonist at the scene of the crime. Or Aunt Millie can't move that piano because at 90 pounds she isn't strong enough.

2. That's when I experiment and play *WHAT IF.* Remember back in an earlier chapter when I suggested you try looking at elements of your story from different angles? Believe me, it's far easier to work out these problems in the scribbling stage than it is after you are some 150 pages into your manuscript.

3. Another aid: I may even throw in a line of dialogue or staple in one of my snapshots. That photograph may save me several hundred words of explanation.

THIRD, I GET ORGANIZED ...

1. Now your task is to get something organized out of all this chaos. In the old days I used 5 x 8 cards. I'd take plot elements that belonged in Chapter One and put them on the first card. Plot elements for Chapter Two went on a second card and so forth. All you're doing here is plucking the elements from your pages of scribbling and making sense of the mishmash. When you do this, you'll discover that some chapters are thin, some a little beefy. Obviously, this is a good place to even things out

2. As I said, this is the way I used to do it. Now I go

through this whole process on my computer and use the editing tools in my software package to accomplish the task for me. If you are one of those fortunate people who can "free think" on a keyboard, this whole organization process can be managed both quicker and easier. If you were in Hollywood, this scene by scene, chapter by chapter arranging and sequencing process would be tantamount to creating a verbal storyboard.

A RECOMMENDATION

Consider this: If the pros in Hollywood (Screen Writers Guild), feel the necessity to map out the plot or outline, maybe that tells you how important this whole phase of the process is regarded. Also, this is probably a good place to mention another little trick. After 13 years and 17 novels, I have learned to estimate the number of pages allowed to tell my story. For sinister fiction I work toward a total of 360 to 380 pages, pretty much of a standard for the paperback "horror" genre. My techno-thrillers run 400 – 450 pages, also a good rule of-thumb. I shoot for 30 – 35 pages per chapter, and depending on the genre, I know how to lay out my chapters.

Therefore, when I sat down to write *Red Tide*, I had a pretty good idea that I was going to need 13 to 15 chapters to tell my story. It may help you to think this way about your manuscript. If you're writing a techno-thriller and you are already to your final conflict scene and you're only at page 267, you may have a problem.

FOURTH, THE PARANOIA DRILL …

1. I spend some time – a couple of hours a day, two or three days max – reviewing what I've got so far. Fresh ideas are added.
2. The garbage is deleted – believe me, there's some stuff in there that doesn't need to be – and I make every effort to tighten up and smooth out the plot.
3. When I'm through and I think I have everything fairly well thought out, I create what I call my *working* outline and start the really fun part of writing my novel, the first draft.

MY EXPERIENCE: Getting ready …

However, before we get into the next chapter, I want to reinforce this advice about getting ready for your journey through a novel. Let me share a story with you.

A number of years ago, while I was still practicing the black art of marketing in the industrial setting, I held a national sales convention in Louisville. I invited a number of people to send me their thoughts on how to be successful, regardless of their field of endeavor.

Bobby Knight, Head Basketball Coach of Indiana University, wrote: *"Lots of people want success; very few people are willing to prepare for success."*

Clive Cussler, author of *Raise the Titanic*, wrote: *"Before I spend nine months writing a novel, I spend nine months getting ready to write nine months."*

John D. MacDonald, prolific author of the incredible Travis McGee series, wrote: *"As far as writing goes, know what you are going to write before you sit down to write."*

Have I made my point? Good, then let's keep going.

45

OUTLINING — THE SHORT LIST

1. **Capture the high points** and tell your story chronologically.

2. **Write down** things that may cause **problems**.

3. Lay out your **major conflicts**.

4. Play **WHAT IF?**

5. Get **organized**.

6. **Review your work daily** for a few days until you're satisfied.

7. **Prepare for success** by getting ready to write before you do it.

FIRST DRAFT — THE FUN PART ...

FIRST: **Write it fast. Get your story started.**

SECOND: **Fix nothing.**

THIRD: **Don't rewrite. Do not go back and fix anything.**

FOURTH: **Have fun.**

Hey, this is what it's all about, storytellers!
Finally, you are ready to write. I mean *really* ready. True, everything you have done up until now is part of the writing process, but now the real fun starts.

When I see a chapter typed on paper for the first time, that's my *first* draft. In that first draft, all I attempt to accomplish is cover everything in that chapter's outline.

A RECOMMENDATION

As you are writing your first draft, you will come upon one of the biggest temptations you'll face as a writer. You will be tempted to go back and start polishing what you've just written. Avoid the temptation. It's a waste of time at this point.

FACT: **By the time you get to the end of your book, your storytelling skills will have improved to such an extent and you will have discovered so many things you omitted, you'll have to go back and rewrite it anyway.**

    I repeat: Don't fix anything. Zip through the rest of your story, all 15 or 20 chapters, all 80,000 to 100,000 words. Get it on paper. This first draft is the one time in your life you don't have to worry about your spelling. The dangling participle is not a concern. Your concern is the story. Is it all there? If it is, congratulations. You have just written a *complete* novel. True, it may not look like you want it to at this point. Making it look like you want it to comes in subsequent drafts.

    So what have you accomplished? Well, for one thing, it is estimated that several million people try to write a novel each year, and the majority of them quit after the first chapter. The other thing you now know for certain is: You did have a story to tell – and you have told it.

WHAT TO DO WHEN YOU'RE THROUGH WITH THE FIRST DRAFT

1.   Ask yourself: Have I achieved my objective?

2.   Compare it to your outline.

3.   Ask yourself: Did I cover everything I had intended to

put in?

4.   Is it all there and in the right sequence?

SUBSEQUENT DRAFTS
No one can tell you how many drafts you are going to have to do to get it right, but I can guarantee you, it will take you more than one.

MY EXPERIENCE: Draft one...
I can't remember why, but I sent a draft of one of my books to my then-agent, Barb Puechner. Barb returned it a couple of weeks later with the comment, "Good idea, Karl. Why don't you develop it and we'll see what it looks like."
Ouch.
Three drafts and six weeks later I sent it back to my agent, got her blessing, and we went on with the project. I had learned a very valuable lesson. A draft is like a fetus; it isn't done yet.

Draft two ...
The first time I did my second draft of a book, I thought it was finished. Wrong! It wasn't. *Red Tide*, my first techno-thriller, went through five drafts – rewrite, editing, final revision, and fine tuning before I mailed it off to my publisher. Don't be surprised if you're sick of your book by the time it's finished. When I finished *Red Tide*, I couldn't wait to get started on the sequel.

REVISING AND EDITING
Okay, so you've resigned yourself to do the necessary revision and editing. The question you're probably asking is how to best go about it? This is what I do. If you find a better and quicker way, write me and tell me all about it.

49

FIRST: START POLISHING …

1.   Starting with page one of your first draft, read and polish.
2.   Do it a chapter at a time.
3.   Look for the trite stuff: cliches, word packages, lazy verbs, poor noun choices (all explained later), typos, misspelled words, and, of course, bad grammar.
4.   After you rewrite each chapter and tighten it, throw away the first version.
5.   Pick at each sentence until you have worked your way through the chapter. (Do I have to tell you you're going to do this with the entire manuscript?)
6.   Don't be afraid to discard material that doesn't work. Just because you typed it on a page doesn't mean you have to keep it.

SECOND: DISCARD AND ADD MATERIAL...

When I'm going through this revision process, I sometimes throw away three or four pages simply because they did nothing for the story. By the same token, I may find where I need to elaborate on some point or where I told the reader about action instead of showing it to him. No matter how much I edit, I seem to end up with more pages in my manuscript than in the first version.

THIRD: LISTEN TO YOUR NOVEL...

FACT: Your ears can 'read' better than you eyes.

Usually, by the end of the second draft, I discover that my story is beginning to look more like the epic I envisioned when I started. Now I'm ready to kick it up a notch. To do that, I haul out my tape recorder and become a reader.

Here's the way it works. Go back to the beginning of your novel, shut off the radio, close the door, and tell the world to go away—you are recording. With no distractions, I carefully read and record five page of my book at a time. When I'm finished working with those five pages, I go to the next five.

When you have every word of those five pages on tape, put your manuscript away, shut your eyes, play your tape, and listen. Be critical. Open your eyes only when you stop your recorder to make a note about something you want to fix.

You will discover that your eyes tend to gloss over mistakes—read things that aren't there or discard words that shouldn't be. You will hear flaws in your manuscript by simply listening to it. What you will hear are all the excess words, the repetitious words, the clumsy words, and the unclear expressions that creep into our writing without our being aware.

FOURTH: MORE DRAFTS...

Now that you have all this garbage isolated, fix it. This trick alone will improve your writing immeasurably. How many times do you do it? Repeat it as many times as necessary to work out the flaws in your mechanics and story construction.

You keep doing it until you're satisfied you can't do anything else to improve the way you've told your story.

NOW WHAT?

Now you show your manuscript to someone. By someone, I mean a professional. Please do not make the mistake of showing it to your mother or your significant other; you want an assessment of your manuscript, not a reaffirmation of their love and concern for you.

51

"Oh, honey, I always knew you were talented."
"You were such a good little writer in the third grade."

Don't even show your novel to friends who are voracious readers. They may know what they like, they may even know what they don't like, but, I'll flat guarantee you, they won't know how to fix something that some editor may consider a fatal flaw.

So who are these professionals? I have a friend in Florida who looked up his old high-school literature teacher. How about that retired English professor in your church? Are you friends with someone who has been published in another field? How about a literary agent? Don't blanch. Sooner or later, an agent becomes part of the scenario. Why not now? Perhaps you met someone at that last writers seminar who would be good at evaluating your manuscript.

I know a young woman, quite talented as a writer, who regularly attends a writer's group. The members read their material to each other and the other members of the group critique. After every meeting she dutifully goes home and makes the recommended changes. She's been working on the same novel for three years and she still can't pull it all together.

My question: Is the criticism valid? Will their suggestions really make it a better book?

You be the judge.

Personally, I think Henry Miller hit the nail on the head when he said, "Artists (that includes novelists) never thrive in colonies ..."

CALISTHENICS

Back at the end of Chapter 3, I asked you to
tell me about your novel. The parameters were
to tell me about your story in 250 keyboarded
words, double-spaced, one page.

Did you do it? Good! That's why you bought
this book, right? You bought it to learn how to
go about writing – and now we add something –
and *selling* your novel.

Now we do the second part of the drill. Reduce
it to 125 words – half of a page, double-spaced.
Trust me, there is a very good reason for doing
this. We'll get to that reason later – in the chapter
on the submission package.

FIRST DRAFT - THE FUN PART – THE SHORT LIST

1.   **Avoid the temptation to go back** and start polishing.

2.   When writing the first draft:

    a.   **Write it fast.**
    b.   **Get your story started**.
    c.   **Fix nothing.**
    d.   **Don't rewrite**.
    e.   **Have fun!**

3.   When you're finished with the first draft:

    a.   **Revise and edit**.
    b.   **Polish.**
    c.   **Discard and add material.**
    d.   **Listen to your novel**.
    e.   **Write another draft**.
    f.   **Repeat above steps as often as necessary to work out the flaws in your mechanics and story construction.**

PLOTS ...

FIRST: A plot is a sequence of events in a story.

SECOND: As a writer, the plot is your plan of action for the characters who will carry out the elements of your story.

THIRD: There are eight crucial elements of a plot.

PLOT OVERVIEW

BEGINNING=EXPOSITION:

1. INTRODUCE CHARACTERS.
   The author introduces most (not necessarily all) of the key characters.
2. GROUND THE READER IN PLACE, TIME AND SETTING.

MIDDLE:

1. PERIOD OF RISING ACTION.
2. PLOT COMPLICATIONS.

CLIMAX:

1. WHERE THE PLOT REACHES MAXIMUM INTENSITY.

END:

1. CONCLUSION=WRAP UP

PLOT STRUCTURE OF COMMERCIAL FICTION

GUIDE TO PLOT ELEMENTS

1.   **The commencement** (getting the show on the road)

2.   **The quandary** (establishing the conflict or problem)

3.   **The commitment** (determination to solve conflict)

4.   **The transition** (move action to location of encounter)

5.   **The encounter** (more than one? Between whom?)

6.   **The moratorium** (importance of ventilating plot)

7.   **The culmination** (showdown or final conflict)

8.   **The consolation** (show 'em what your protagonist won)

The commencement ...

Obviously, this is the first component of your plot. This is where you get the ball rolling. To get the ball rolling, you should plan on meeting several objectives. Why? Because you are trying to achieve several things:
You want to create a sense of mood
You want to create a sense of place
You want to create a sense of time
And most important
You want to grab the reader – set the hook.

Your task in the commencement is to introduce some of the critical elements of your story – a crime, a romance, a conflict, a problem to be solved – whatever is the theme of your story. Let me give you an example.

In *Red Wind*, the fourth book in my *Red* series, the opening paragraph describes a homicide inspector in Kiev (Ukraine) stumbling through the darkened, nearly flooded backstreets of a prop lot in an old abandoned movie studio to investigate the murder of an unidentified woman. In approximately 28 words the reader gets a feel for time, place, and mood. The hook is set.

Let's try another example – this one from *The Pond*, written under one of my pseudonyms, Simon Lawrence.

Milo Adcock was born on a sultry July evening in the year 1945, unattended in a third-rate Biloxi motel. His mother, May Belle Adcock, was all of 14 at the time, a sharecropper's daughter, unschooled and possessed of limited mental capacities.

Does it meet the tests described above? It comes close. The commencement of your novel should be tightly written and present the reader with an intriguing first peek into the adventure you are about to unfold. Remember this: The commencement is the baseline of your novel. You are establishing a pace, fully aware that as your story unfolds, that pace must be ever accelerating.

1. How long should the commencement be?
2. How soon do I have to introduce my protagonist (hero, heroine, or both) in the commencement?

Answer to the first question: Your commencement can be as long as you want it to be. You don't have to achieve everything in the first couple of paragraphs, but don't dilly-dally either. There are all too many readers out there who, if you don't hook them in the first couple of paragraphs you may lose them. Unfair? Yup, but there isn't much you can do about it except hook them early.

Answer to the second question: I happen to believe that getting the reader into the plot is the most important thing I can do to hook the reader in a techno-thriller. I try to do that as quickly as possible. The philosophy? Don't drag the reader into your story, catapult them into it. I want the reader thinking, *"How the hell can this situation possibly be solved?"* Only then do I introduce the character who is going to solve it.

How far have I gone into my story before introducing my protagonist? Sometimes ten, sometimes twenty pages. However, I have, in some of my sinister fiction novels, introduced him in the first paragraph. Want examples? In *Jaws*, Peter Benchley's blockbuster novel about a great white shark, the shark devours a young woman before you are introduced to Sheriff Brody (first the problem, then you meet the hero). In *Sunset Boulevard*, the opening paragraph begins with the words of one of the protagonists. Talk about hook, the character saying those lines is already dead.

PITFALL

There is a tendency for beginning novelists to try to overwhelm the reader with information about their hero or heroine when they introduce the primary character (hero, heroine, protagonist). Don't do that. Forget the idea of planting an instant personnel file in the reader's mind. Start with essential detail and feed the reader a continual supply of

information that will help the character grow in
the reader's mind. Why? Because that's the way
we learn about people in real life. If we dumped
all the facts about ourselves on that first date, there
would be no second date.

The quandary ...

This is where you present your protagonist with the
problem. Simple? No way. The problem is fraught with
consequences. Example: The protagonist receives a call from a
presidential staffer who says, "The president wants you to go to
Greenland. One of our planes is down, and the wreckage has
slid under an ice shelf. It's packing a fused nuclear weapon, and
we need your help to retrieve it."

Hey, this guy is supposed to be a hero, right? So what's
the quandary? Well, he is about to reconcile with his wife who
left him because he is always putting his job before his marriage.
He loves this woman and it has taken him a long time to
convince her that she should give him one more chance.

Or how about Sheriff Brody in *Jaws*? If he opens the
beaches, he is taking a risk; the shark may kill even more
victims. If he closes the beaches, the resort community stands a
good chance of going bankrupt; those 90 days of summer are
critical to the resort island community's economic survival.

A RECOMMENDATION
Never make the hero's choice obvious or
easy. The choice should be painful. The
less clear the decision, the more interest-
sustaining the quandary will be.

59

In this matter of the quandary, I think it gives the character dimension to have the protagonist vacillate. Why? It adds suspense. Your reader can relate to having to make difficult choices. One more thing: Never have your hero ruminate on a decision between right and wrong. The reader will wonder if your character has the right set of moral and ethical values. When you present your quandary, it should be between two rights or the lesser of two wrongs.

BREAK TIME

This is probably a good time to take a break, make a few notes, reflect on what we have discussed about the elements of plot, and revisit your decision about writing a novel. If you are still enthused and chomping at the bit, let's move on to the next plot element.

The commitment ...

Our techno-thriller protagonist receives a second call. This one is from the president himself: "Be at the airport at fifteen hundred hours. I'm sending Air Force Two to pick you up."

Oh, boy. What's this guy going to tell his wife?

A RECOMMENDATION

Make the commitment sticky ... it adds intrigue and keeps the reader turning pages to find out what happens.

One thing you can count on: Your protagonist will be

condemned for choosing either course of action. But – and this is important – you, as author, have several hundred pages in which he can redeem himself. **The key to a good quandary is to make the choice difficult.**

The transition ...

"Transition from what?" someone is asking. The transition is where you shift the scene from the everyday world of your hero to the place where the main action takes place. In the case of our techno-thriller protagonist, he is transported from the airport in his hometown to the wastelands of the Arctic. How's that for a change of setting?

Putting people in motion is important. There is a sense of adventure in travel, particularly when you can begin to describe the desolate, barren, forbidding Arctic terrain. Not only that, you can make the journey fraught with peril. Add even more adventure; let him crash land in some inhospitable region where he is the only survivor. Now your hero, out of contact with civilization, stranded, alone and maybe even injured, has to save himself before he can solve the perils of the armed nuclear weapon under the ice shelf. This is the kind of stuff that keeps your reader panting. With a plane crash this early in the book, it's a pretty good indication the hero's life is going to be pure hell before this saga is over.

I don't believe the value of a solid transition element can be overstated. The transition portion of your story accomplishes so many things. This is where you increase the tempo. This is where your plot points begin to materialize at an even faster pace. This is where you create new and unexpected impediments for your hero to overcome. This is, for example, where a reader discovers someone high up in the president's administration is trying to impede the hero's progress by sabotaging his plane. The plot thickens; which is exactly what is supposed to happen at this point in your story's development.

Exciting? You bet.

The encounter ...

Since I sat down to write my book on writing, I've learned a little more about this particular element of the plot. Back when I listed the encounter as the fifth element, I failed to mention that when you outline this particular phase of your novel, you are, in all likelihood, going to want to include more than one encounter. So, as you outline this part of your story, you may actually want to indicate something like encounter #1, encounter #2, encounter #3, etc.

How many? Who knows? I know it takes more than one. Why? Because it builds tension in your plot to have more than one encounter between the forces of good and the forces of evil. (Force of evil = bad guy = antagonist).

Let me explain. Again I will use an example from *Jaws*. If you will recall, the protagonist (Sheriff Brody) and the antagonist (the shark) do not actually have a face-to-face encounter until all three men, Quint, Hooper, and Brody, have boarded the *Orca* (which was the transition element in the story). When they have that first encounter, it is a brief one; Brody sees the shark for the first time and realizes how big the shark is. In the second encounter, Quint (not Brody) attempts to keep the beast from sounding by harpooning it and tying barrels to its back. In the third encounter, the shark rams the *Orca* and punches a hole in the side. The fourth encounter is the climax. Brody kills the shark.

You, as a beginning author, should understand what is happening here. The first encounter was more psychological than physical. For the first time, Brody realizes the magnitude of the undertaking. True, the second encounter is only viewed by Brody, but he now sees the task of getting rid of the shark as even more daunting than he did before. The third encounter is physical, pure brute force, and, in a manner of speaking, the shark wins the third encounter; he has punched a hole in the hull of the *Orca*. Of course, Brody wins in the end, but by then your reader is breathless – and that's what you want.

If you go back and read the above paragraph a second time, you'll see that the author of *Jaws* is doing something else here; *each successive encounter escalates the action*. Each successive encounter makes the reader think that Brody's eventual victory over the beast is more and more in question. In other words, keep your reader guessing: Will he or won't he win? One way to do this, of course, is to let the antagonist (villain) win one of the encounters. When the shark punches a hole in the hull of Quint's boat, you have to give that round to the shark.

It really doesn't matter how you portray the initial encounter, but you need to remember two things:

1. The first encounter, as well as the ones that follow, should give your reader some indication of the magnitude of the ultimate conflict that lies ahead.

2. Each successive encounter should be more intense than the previous confrontation between your elements of good and evil, in most cases, the hero and the villain.

The moratorium ...

The moratoriums are brief. In a line of dashes, it is a dot. In a line of dots, it is a dash.

Why do we need moratoriums? Because in your effort to ever increase the intensity, playing each note higher, you will eventually hear your reader say, "Gimme a break. Back off. You're not giving me a chance to breathe."

To understand the moratorium, you need to think a moment about pace and rhythm. Some writers seem to have trouble grasping the concept. Others master this subtlety early on. One of the best is Stephen King. You can learn a great deal about this element of plotting by studying Stephen King's cadence. In my opinion, he is the master of story telling rhythm. Ta-da, ta-da, ta-da, boom! Compound sentence, compound sentence, compound sentence, simple declarative sentence. Compare this to the first four notes in Beethoven's Fifth Symphony, da da da daaaaa – or the S.O.S. code, dot dot dot dash. It sounds like a technique that's easy to master, but, like so many other components of writing a good, reader-friendly, commercial piece of fiction, it takes practice. More practice for some than others.

The moratorium scenes are ones that you build into your plot to allow the reader to relax. You place them between highly dramatic scenes, keeping in mind that they must fit within the context of your story. They are used for the express purpose of what professionals call, *ventilating* the plot – allowing readers to catch their breath.

An excellent example of a plot moratorium (ventilation) can be found in the scene aboard the *Orca* in *Jaws* when Quint, Brody, and Hooper are sitting in the galley drinking beer and singing. (Hey, I know it sounds like a crazy thing to be doing under the circumstances, but it is typical macho male behavior.) That moratorium scene fits nicely between the second and third encounter with the shark. Your reader not only gets a chance to breathe a little deeper, the reader may even laugh.

If you still haven't grasped the concept of plot ventilation, grab a couple of John D. MacDonald books, go through them and note how many times he uses this device – a conversation, a reflection while polishing the teak on the *Busted Flush*, etc.

The culmination ...

This is it. The high point. The big scene. Probably the one you had in mind when you started this endeavor. If you are a romance writer, this is where your lovers finally overcome all obstacles and get together. If you are writing a mystery, this is where the mystery is solved. This is where good conquers evil. This is where the nasty gunslinger finally loses. This is where our techno-thriller hero finally defuses the nuclear device on the plane under the ice shelf.

I feel certain I don't have to tell you this: It should be the most exciting part of your book. This is where everything culminates. You've gone from big, to bigger, to boffo. This is where you put on your most dazzling display of fireworks. This is where you want your reader to say, "Wow." In *Red Wind* I had the helicopter trying to get the president (who has just had a near fatal heart attack and was already on a life-support system) to the helipad atop the hospital while being chased by terrorists in another chopper. Not exciting enough, you say. All this was happening while an ice storm had paralyzed the entire city, communications were out, and another team of terrorists had stationed themselves in strategic locations where they could destroy the president's chopper in the event it somehow made it through all the other obstacles. Still not enough? The choppers collide and the flaming wreckage falls on the roof of the hospital. Now my protagonist, already injured, has to claw his way through flaming debris to try to save the president. That's what I mean by *big scene*.

And since I've used *Jaws* in other examples, the culmination is where Brody, alone now on the sinking *Orca*, climbs up the antenna to get one last shot at the giant shark.

Will evil triumph? Of course not. But let me remind you that you are the one who put your protagonist through all this misery. Now you have to find a way to extricate him.

IMPORTANT
Don't fall into the trap of killing off your hero.

Having said that, perhaps I better elaborate on a point that always comes up in my seminars. It comes up all too frequently not to mention it.

Someone will say something like, "I don't want good to triumph over evil. I want the dark side to win." If that's your intention, you would be smart to rethink your plot.

Why? Because in study after study, readers have indicated they don't like dark endings. Consider this: A reader really gets into your story and devotes a couple of hours of precious time each night to your book. The reader gets involved with your characters. In other words, that reader has an emotional investment. Readers sympathize with your characters. And what do you do? You kill off the character he really cared about.

Shame, double shame on you. If you must kill off your protagonist and your story won't work any other way, put that story away and write it only after you have authored – and published – hot-selling other works. A dark ending needs a strong editor in your corner who will go to bat for you at the editorial meeting, and enough readers to insure they will tolerate that kind of story culmination – and keep buying your books.

Let me conclude this section on plot culmination with a couple of other comments. The rhythm in your writing plays a big part in pulling off a socko culmination. Every word must contribute to the scene. No moratoriums during the culmination. In showdowns there are no wasted motions. That means no wasted words. Survival is at stake. Action is paramount. Never was the old adage, "show, don't tell," more important.

Let me offer this advice about authoring your first novel: Stick to a single story line. Avoid the temptation to include too many complicated subplots and complex, subtle relationships. Generally speaking, the moment you step up from a simple story line, you are inviting writing problems. They may well be problems you are not yet equipped to handle.

PLOTS – THE SHORT LIST

1.   **A plot is a sequence of events** in a story.

      Beginning
      Middle
      Climax
      Conclusion

2.   **The plot is your plan of action for the characters** who will carry out the elements of your story.

3.   The **8 plot elements** consist of:

      The commencement
      The quandary
      The commitment
      The transition
      The encounter
      The moratorium
      The culmination
      The consolation

4.   **Don't fall into the trap of killing off your hero.**

TITLES ...

FIRST: **First time authors seldom have title approval.**

SECOND: **Titles should be short and snappy.**

DON'T FALL IN LOVE WITH YOUR TITLE...

You could spend a good part of your life examining the art of coming up with a title that sells a book. If you should happen to discover the way to create a can't-miss title, you could retire rich.

MY EXPERIENCES: Fifty percent ...

My own track record for writing titles that end up on my books is spotty at best. I just fired off my seventeenth novel to my publisher. I titled it *The Jakarta Plot*, but heaven only knows what title it will be published under. Of the sixteen prior novels, eight were printed with the suggested (read that, **my**) title. For instance, my novel, *The Lake*, was written under the title *The Mist*. *Pagoda* was submitted under the title *The Ultimates*.

"TITLES SHOULD BE SHORT AND SNAPPY"

This is a direct quote from my publisher. This makes it easy to understand a Dick Francis title like *Whip Hand* or *Longshot*. It does not account for something like *Silence of the Lambs*. It isn't short. It isn't snappy. And who can explain the titles of Robert Ludlum's works? Perhaps fans of those authors see the author's name and buy the book, regardless of title.

YOU CAN'T GENERALIZE OR MAKE RULES, BUT...

Titles defy generalizations, let alone rules, but I do have some thoughts you should consider when you are naming your first book. So let me say the following and you decide from there, okay?

1.   Most editors don't care for titles that use made-up words. One of my former editors suggests that first novelists stick to familiar words that don't have to be explained in the course of the story. In my book, *The Witch of Sixkill*, the witch came from the village of Sixkill. They used that one.

2.   The same editor also suggests avoiding using foreign words and dates in the title. The theory here is that many people won't know what the title means or that the material is dated for reprints. Sure, *1984* is an exception.

3.   That editor goes on to say a good, clear title helps them position the book. Editors are thinking about cover art when they are evaluating how your book will be marketed.

4.   Finally, while celebrities and best-selling authors usually have title approval, first time authors seldom do.

So, title your endeavor as you wish, but don't be surprised if they tell you they want to change it.

TITLES – THE SHORT LIST

1.   Titles should be **short, clear and snappy**.

2.   Titles **defy rules**.

3.   Most editors don't care for:
        a.   **Made – up words**.
        b.   **Foreign words**.
        c.   **The use of dates**.

4.   First time authors **seldom have title approval**.

STYLE ...

FIRST: Style is not *what* you write; it is *how* you write.

SECOND: Style is form, not content.

THIRD: Don't be verbose, sesquipedalianistic, or wordy.

MY DEFINITION:
A writing style is something distinctly different from the idea being expressed. Your writing style is the way you as an author express thoughts, visions, scenes, or any other component of your written work. Let me come at it from a different angle: An author's style is his or her characteristic way of writing. It becomes your uniqueness and distinctiveness when you tell a story. Expressed still another way, it is the excellence (or lack of it), the originality (or lack of same), and the character (not characters) of your written expression.

DON'T GET HUNG UP ON STYLE
Now you know what style is, but that doesn't tell you what you need to know to write a commercial novel. Suffice to say this — **Be yourself**. If you write naturally and honestly, your own unique style will come through.

Voltaire said, "Any style that is not boring is good."

Take the hint. Don't be boring and you'll do just fine.

A RECOMMENDATION

Let me give you a couple of examples of style, both successful. Pick up a copy of Jay Anson's, *The Amityville Horror*. Some 23 million people have read it. Most of the people I talk to read it in one sitting, not because it is short, but because it is a gripping, fascinating study in horror. That, my friend, is commercial writing.

Then, when you are through with that, tackle Gertrude Stein's *Three Lives*. The challenge here is to try to stay awake through three pages. This is not the style of commercial fiction. It may be literary and they may love it in the lit survey classes in American universities, but it is not the sort of thing people are lining up to buy in bookstores.

Heed Voltaire. If you keep falling asleep while you are reading and editing your manuscript, you may have a problem.

GUIDES TO THE COMMERCIAL STYLE OF WRITING

FACT: There are no strict rules in style.

No one can tell you how to express or describe something in words. On the other hand, if your style is not appropriate for commercial fiction, there are some cautions you should heed.

How do you know if your style is boring, you ask?

Here are some clues. People fall asleep. Your boss nods off. Your wife tries to change the subject. Your dog yawns. If you have experienced any of these, your style needs polishing. Here are some very practical guidelines that will help you improve.

GUIDELINES

1. DON'T BE VERBOSE ...

If your style is verbose, you are overdoing the pretentious and flowery words and phrases.
A VERBOSE STYLE IS THE STYLE OF AN AMATEUR

Somewhere along the line, beginning novelists think that writing a novel means using lots of words. Not true. You don't write lots of words, you tell a story. And, if you are doing it correctly, you will use only the words your story requires.

It's time to take stock. If you complete your novel and it only adds up to 45,000 words instead of the 120,000 you anticipated, maybe you didn't have a big enough story for a novel in the first place.

Remember the example of Gertrude Stein's *Three Lives*?

Let me pass along a tip from no less a master than Rod Serling: **LESS WORDS IS MORE BETTER**. So saying, he went on to explain that, in general, the fewer words you use in a sentence, the greater impact that sentence will have on the reader. Using too many big, ungainly, unfamiliar words will lose more readers than they will impress

2. DON'T BE SESQUIPEDALIANISTIC ...

Don't try to dazzle your readers with a plethora of big words. You are not trying to impress a professor; you are trying to entertain a reader.

3. DON'T BE WORDY ...

Wordy writers crank out long, ungainly, over-written sentences and often lose the reader in a confusing maze of words.

A RECOMMENDATION

Get the garbage out of your writing. Definition of garbage: Words you don't need. Getting the garbage out of your writing takes practice.

CALISTHENICS

Rewrite this sentence: The people caught in the rain at the parade got wet. (11 words)

What's wrong with that you ask? Well, did you notice the redundancy? ... **caught in the rain** and **got wet**. What about the word wet? Could you use a better word and give the reader more information? Maybe it would be better if you wrote **drenched** or **soaked**. When you do, you've painted a more precise word picture without cluttering up your sentence.

So, instead of writing a sentence full of garbage (verbosity), you write something like *Rain drenched everyone at the parade*. Six words: Cleaner, neater, and it gives the reader even more information – how wet did they get?

PARASITES THAT SUCK THE LIFE OUT OF GOOD WRITING
FIRST: UNNECESSARY WORDS (REDUNDANCIES)

CALISTHENICS

Find the unnecessary words in the following sentences:
She rode a three-wheeled tricycle.
Red blood gushed from the wound.
She placed a single block on top of the pile.
He was strangled to death on the mattress of his bed.

The first sentence is obvious. How many wheels does a tricycle usually have? It's safe to assume most readers know the difference between a bicycle and tricycle.

The second sentence is equally obvious. Red? Blood? What color is blood? Okay, okay, so you're writing about an alien. In that case the editor might buy green blood.

The third sentence is really bad. Block is singular. So why say single block? In addition, the sentence includes the article "a" which is likewise singular. In this sentence you have a redundancy piled on top of a redundancy.

Finally, in the fourth sentence you have the word strangled, which includes by definition death. And, since mattresses are usually on beds, it can be boiled down to: He was strangled on his mattress.

SECOND: EMPTY WORDS

Another style of no-no writing revolves around the use of empty words. Empty words modify words which require no modification. Have you ever heard someone say, "This is almost impossible?" Sure you have. A good writer would not write "almost impossible" unless one of his or her characters was using this awkward phrase in straight dialogue. If it's impossible, it's impossible. Why say "almost impossible" when you mean, very difficult? Bottom line: You cannot modify an absolute. It either is or isn't.

How about the phrase "pretty good"? In this case the word good is not an absolute. It is a personal evaluation. The word pretty is a descriptive term. Do they go together? Not really. Ask yourself: Does the reader have more information just because you threw the word pretty in there? I can think of cases where you might use this phrase in a line of dialogue, but not narrative. Incidentally, the word good is a weak word. There are 235 synonyms for the word good. Which one did you have in mind?

Would you say your mother's cooking is good, or would delicious, tasty, delectable, scrumptious, appetizing, or even palatable be more accurate and informative?

THIRD: HELPLESS WORDS ...

Finally, we come to the weak words that need modifiers. The only thing to do with helpless words is to get rid of them. Find stronger, more accurate, more definitive words to take their place.

One of the best ways to search out helpless words is to look for words ending in –ly. An editor once told me that one of the quickest and easiest ways to see evidence of a rookie writer was their frequent use of –ly words. Do you have your protagonist running quickly when he could have been sprinting? Can you find characters in your story who are smiling happily or speaking softly? Why don't you just say smiling? Is a smiling person unhappy? As for speaking softly, the word whispering is stronger, more descriptive, and gives the reader more information with fewer words.

PITFALL
Weak writers rely on –ly words.

CALISTHENICS

Here's a short drill you can do to make you more
aware of this problem with helpless words. Find
precise verbs to replace the following:

Walked quickly could be _____

Walked aimlessly could be _____

Kissed lightly could be _____

Breathed deeply could be _____

Every time you replace a weak verb and adverb combination
with a strong single verb, you are improving your style. Editors
are looking for writers who have mastered the art of tight, fast-
paced storytelling.

CALISTHENICS

Reduce the number of words in each sentence
without depriving the reader of relevant information.

1. Robert Miller was a soft-spoken professor who frowned
    repeatedly when he was describing the assassination of
    President John Kennedy that fateful day in Dallas. (25
    words)
2. Amish puzzles are difficult to solve. (6 words)
3. William Peter Blatty's novel, *The Exorcist*, is generally
    considered to be the finest example of modern American
    horror fiction. (19 words)

No answers this time. You're on your own. Trust me, there is
plenty of garbage in the above. Take it out. Revise. Edit.
Write like a pro.

A RECOMMENDATION
Learn to search out the word that gives the
reader the most information and says exactly
what you mean.

REVISING AND EDITING

Those of you who happen to be golfers as well as
writers are probably familiar with that old expression *drive for
show, putt for dough.* For our purposes, let's change that to
write for show, revise for dough.

Knowing how to revise and edit can make the difference
between a novel that sells and one that doesn't. If I could sit at
your elbow while you are going through the editing and revising
process, I'm convinced I could show you where, even with a
well-developed outline, your manuscript is weighted down with
purposeless words.

One colleague of mine likes to say, "Writing is over-
rated. You make your money writing commercial fiction during
the revision process." I agree.

First, get your whole story on paper. Then make it
sparkle and glisten. How? By polishing your literary gem until
it is as professional as you can possibly make it. When you
learn to do this, you've taken another giant stride toward
becoming a professional.

WRITING REMINDERS:
1.Find the right word.
2.Learn to write tight.

After seventeen novels, five *how-to* books, and over six-hundred weekly newspaper columns, I still need that occasional reminder that if I want my work to *sing*, I have to spend twice as much time editing and revising as I do developing that first draft.

WRITE TIGHT: VERBS

Just to get the hang of learning to write tight, let's start with action words. Burn this one into your brain:

1.   Always use the strongest verb to get the job done.

EXAMPLE ONE: He *walked* to the park to meet his contact.

Now, ask yourself, how else could you describe the process of how this ambulatory character got to the park? Start with the realization that you have a great many choices. How about: *step, amble, stride, pace, tread, foot it, slog, trudge, plod, shamble, shuffle, stagger, wobble, waddle, sidle, slink, proceed, promenade, hike, tramp,* or even *march.*
Obviously, some of the synonyms listed above won't work for one reason or another, but depending on your character's mind-set as he heads for the park, you certainly can come up with a stronger word than *walk.*

EXAMPLE TWO: *She cried.*

I know what you're thinking. How are you going to get

any tighter than two words? The thing that is wrong with *she cried* is it is pure vanilla. Think of other possibilities: *wept, bawled, blubbered, whimpered, whined, wailed, moaned, groaned,* and *lamented.* Ask yourself if any of these alternatives give the reader a better word picture.

Let me demonstrate how this could work in the context of an actual scene from a novel. The scene is a courtroom. Your protagonist is on the stand, testifying in a sexual harassment case. The lawyer asks your protagonist what happened and she responds, "He *touched* me." (At least it is tight writing.) But how much more powerful would it have been if she had said, "He *pawed* me." *Pawed* is far more descriptive and informative than *touched.* Not only that, it has a great deal more impact.

Mastery of this facet of writing alone will elevate your writing several notches and help you capture one more degree of professionalism.

WRITE TIGHT: NOUNS

Everything we've just said about verbs applies to nouns as well. In your first novel, your style will improve every time you use a precise, concrete noun in place of a general, imprecise one.

CALISTHENICS

Try this little drill. Open your manuscript, any page. See how many nouns you can replace with a more precise one. When you see a sentence that reads something like "Tommy is a crook," see how much more information you are giving the reader when you write "Tommy is an arsonist." or, "Tommy is a murderer." In each example, the reader knows a great deal more about Tommy.

If you write, "Betty ate breakfast," the reader knows what happened. If you write, "Betty ate cereal,." the reader knows even more. But if you write, "Betty ate oatmeal," your reader has even more information than in the second version.

See how specific you can be without being wordy when you construct a sentence? Did Sharon eat dinner? Did Sharon eat meat? Did Sharon eat steak? Did Sharon eat filet mignon?

FIND THE RIGHT WORD

Tighten your writing by using **strong nouns rather than adding an adjective.**

I can hear some of you now:

For crying out loud, Largent, what's wrong with adjectives? Answer: Not a thing. But adjectives (words that modify nouns) have a way of becoming a crutch for a lazy writer.

A RECOMMENDATION
A rule of thumb: Use adjectives only when there is no other way to achieve the effect you want. In other words, use an adjective only when you are making a conscious decision to use an adjective.

Why write a *little stone* when you mean a *pebble*? Why write *very beautiful* when you mean *stunning*? Why write *really hungry* when you mean *famished*? Learn to get a death grip on your vocabulary and start squeezing it until the right word drops out.

SHOW ACTION
Learn to develop a style that *shows* action ...

MY EXPERIENCE: Show, don't tell ...
After completing the final draft of *The Prometheus Project*, a novel about an attempt to locate a Nazi doomsday device lying at the bottom of the Caribbean, I fired the manuscript off to New York. Within two weeks, my editor had fired it back accompanied by a two-page, single-spaced letter outlining several changes he wanted me to make. Among those "suggested" (on your first novel you better make 'em when your editor "suggests") changes was a scene about a third of the way into the book. In the original version, Elliott Wages (my protagonist) after a night-long and unsuccessful effort to

84

save a salvage barge from sinking, goes back to his cabin to get some much needed sleep. He has been asleep only a short time when Hanna comes to his cabin to break the news that the barge has sunk.

The original scene was written this way:

I heard Hanna's footsteps in the passageway. She pushed the door open, studied me for a moment; and sagged down on my bunk. Her eyes were bloodshot and she appeared exhausted. I knew what had happened without her telling me.

"We lost it," she said. "There was nothing we could do."

The rewrite of that scene follows. It is a good example of showing action, not telling the reader about it after the fact. As you can see, the scene reads entirely different and is much stronger. (Note, I even changed characters from the lovely Hanna to a couple of deck hands aboard the *Slo Gin*.)

"Wake up, mon," Queet yelled.

I stared up into the semi-darkness at the shiny face looking down at me. Sarge was right behind him.

"Go away," I grumbled.

"You better come topside," Queet warned.

There was something in his voice that told me this was no time to roll back over and try to pick up the fragmented pieces of my vaguely erotic dream. I pushed back the sheet, shoved my aching legs over the edge of the bed, and struggled to my feet. By the time I had everything working and headed for the deck, Queet had already explained what was happening. The <u>Bay Foreman</u> *was sinking hard by the stern. She had already assumed a near 45 degree angle in the water. The two salvage hoists, despite their height, were all but submerged.*

The commotion was enough to bring the entire crew topside. We viewed the last minutes of the creaking old barge with a kind of stoic resignation. We had purposely refrained from removing the crew's bodies the previous night so that we could get a better idea of what had happened in the harsh light of day. Now that opportunity was gone. The residue of whatever catastrophe had befallen the ship was now floating in the swirling waters around the reef.

"Damn, mon," Queet muttered, "that's the sound I heard all through the night. It was that old ship a dyin'."

The Bay Foreman hadn't gone quietly. In the still boiling, debris-littered waters that swallowed her up, she sounded like an old woman struggling, gasping for her last breath. When the exhaust stacks disappeared, there was a final protest against the assault of the invading waters.

Because she didn't go quietly, she brought on the predators. At first it was only a couple of small tiger sharks, but Sarge kept spotting newcomers. Finally, a massive 14-footer emerged from the turbulence off of the stern, his lethal body sandpapering the hull of the Slo Gin as he circled through the remaining bloated bodies of the Foreman's crew. When the giant jerked the last of those bodies beneath the surface, it was all over.

See the difference? There are a couple of things I should point out here. First, you can see the obvious difference between telling and showing. The reader gets a far more vivid picture of what is happening aboard the *Slo Gin* in the second version. Second, you can also see how adding this passage alters the text. Even though you have been busy editing those garbage words out of your manuscript, you can see how the text can be expanded by elaborating on some event you may have given only minimal attention in an earlier draft. Scenes where you have *told* the reader instead of *showing* the reader the action are just one more aspect of storytelling you need to learn to guard against when you are revising and editing.

Whatever you do, avoid the temptation to gloss over a scene because you haven't experienced anything like it in real life.

STYLE – THE SHORT LIST

1. Style is **not *what* you write**; it is *how* **you write**.

2. Remember, it's *form*, *not content*.

3. **Don't be verbose** – pretentious or flowery.

4. **Don't be sesquipedalianistic** – no big words.

5. **Don't be wordy** – don't overwrite.

6. **Avoid unnecessary words** – redundancies.

7. **Avoid empty words** – don't modify absolutes.

8. Avoid helpless words – pick the right word.

9. **Revise, edit,** and learn to **write tight.**

MORE ON STYLE ...

FIRST: **Avoid being a "lazy writer."**

SECOND: **There are several different approaches to the use of attributes.**

THIRD: **The key to good style is to polish, edit, revise and tighten.**

CLICHES AND WORD PACKAGES

Editors can spot a rookie—read that "a lazy writer"—by the number of times the writer resorts to cliches and word packages. Sure, it's easy to write:

Behind the eight ball
Hit the nail on the head
Black as night

... and a thousand more. Never, I repeat, never use a cliché or word package in your narrative. Don't do it—with one exception. On occasion—and seldom at that, you can have a character use it in a line of dialogue. After all, we try to make our characters (at least the human ones) as human as possible and, as we all know, humans often resort to the use of cliches and word packages.

APPEAL TO ALL THE SENSES

One of the more frequent sins committed by new writers is their habit of appealing only to the sense of sight. They can create marvelous scenes of sunsets, gray dawn, good-looking women, shiny cars, neon-bathed streets, and on and on. But what happened to the rest of the senses? Surely your characters, as well as your readers, are used to exercising more than just the sense of sight.

If we can believe what we read, we are told that one of the things that separates us from the rest of the animal kingdom is the fact that we have developed the entire constellation of senses. There are creatures that see better, smell better, hear better, but, on balance, we do all of them better as an integrated package.

So, why do new writers always focus on how everything looks?

CALISTHENICS

Here's a little drill that will bring home this point. Your protagonist, a beautiful woman, intelligent and ambitious, has been informed that she can find the answer to the whereabouts of her long missing father in an old abandoned crypt. It is night. The wind is howling. There is thunder in the distance. It's starting to rain as she enters the windowless crypt. Suddenly the door slams shut behind her. She drops her flashlight. It breaks. She is surrounded by darkness.

Now, tell me what she sees? Right. She can't see squat. She can't describe what it looks like—the texture of the walls, the shape of the coffin, nothing. It's pitch black in there. In fact, the only thing she can rely on are her other senses. And at this point she is having a whole cadre of sensations, isn't she?

I'll bet you would if you were caught in the same situation.

Hey, budding author types, at the very least, she is nervous. She may even be terrified. Is she sweating? Is she having trouble breathing? Is her throat constricted?

There are lots of things going on with this woman at this moment. What are they? You created her. You know her better than anyone else. So what is she experiencing?

WHAT DOES SHE **HEAR?**
  The howling wind?
  The deathly silence inside the crypt?
  The beat of her own heart? Her pulse?
  An unidentified rustling?

WHAT DOES SHE **SMELL?**
  Staleness?
  Mildew?
  Rot?
  Decay?

WHAT DOES SHE **TASTE?**
  Has her mouth gone dry?
  What does fear taste like?

91

WHAT IS SHE **THINKING?**
(Besides I wish to hell I could get out of here.)
Is she frightened?
Terrified?
Apprehensive
Brave?
Determined?

To write this kind of scene, or any scene involving our responses, both physical and emotional, to unfamiliar stimuli, you must remember that all the senses come into play. Your character is experiencing *something*; what is it? As a storyteller you are doing a good job when the reader experiences the same emotions and sensations your character is feeling.

A RECOMMENDATION
When you write, remember: Appeal to all the senses. It's worth repeating what Stephen King said: "When I tell a story, my intent is to scare the hell out of you." And in case it hasn't happened to you lately, being scared is definitely a total sensory experience.

That's enough about writing to all the senses. Let's move now to a writing arena where there is some controversy.

ATTRIBUTIONS
There are several different approaches to this matter of attributes. But first I would be remiss if I did not define an attribution as a writer thinks of it. Writers use the word *attribution* to define both the source and the words spoken by a character.

Example: "Don't shoot," she said. In this example the words *she said* is the attribution.

FIRST: THE DAME AGATHA CHRISTIE APPROACH...

Simply stated, she seldom uses attributions. In a Christie novel, you will often find pages of dialogue without an indication of who said what or how the line was delivered. This, my friends, takes a skilled writer. I have heard more than one person complain about getting lost in who was saying what to whom in a Christie novel. Also, there is the matter of writing a scene in which more than one person is talking. Some attributes—even for Agatha Christie—are a must in a scene involving more than two characters.

One final word on how the great lady handles attributes: If you could write like Agatha Christie and had her legions of readers, you probably wouldn't be reading this handbook.

SECOND: OTHER AUTHORS...

Many espouse a totally different view of this subject of attributions. They are the authors who claim the word *said* is totally invisible. They believe the word to be so imperceptible that it won't be distracting to the reader. You can use it, they say, as often as you want to and it won't be confusing. They even go so far as to say words like *added, continued*, and *argued* are tip-offs that the writer is an amateur unable to grasp a more professional style. (That statement is a bit strong for my taste.)

They also say body language isn't audible. That words like *sneer, grin,* or *snort*, cannot be heard and therefore cannot be used as attributions. (If you've ever heard someone snort, I'm sure you will agree it is a very audible sound. My uncle can't tell a joke without snorting.)

Arguments for only using *said* as an attribution are built around their belief that your dialogue should be strong enough to carry the emotion in the voice. On this one point, they get no argument from me. But again, I believe they are being too pedantic. Let's go back to the statement at the beginning of the chapter on style, namely, *there are no rules, only guidelines.* Proponents of the use only of the word *said* would be wise to remember that.

THIRD: THOSE AUTHORS WHO BELIEVE IN USING A NUMBER OF ATTRIBUTIONS...

Last, of course, is the school of writing that believes a writer should be able to use any of the vast number of attributions available to the storyteller. Sometimes it isn't necessary to use an attribution at all. Sometimes the word *said* is sufficient. And there are occasions when you as the storyteller are justified in writing a line of dialogue that reads something like, *"We can't go on this way," she cried.* What's wrong with that? Nothing. The one thing you don't want to do is hang an adverb like the word *angrily* on the sentence after the word *cried.* If the word *cried* isn't strong enough to carry both the response and the way the dialogue was delivered, maybe you need a better verb.

IT'S YOUR STYLE...

The bottom line to all of this is, it's your style and you

are the one who has to decide how you are going to handle attributions. The above discussion should serve no other purpose than to serve as a guideline.

DICTATES OF YOUR STYLE...

Let me bring this chapter to a close with this: The key to a good, crisp, and effective style is to polish, edit, revise, and tighten. Those four steps, plus your uniqueness of expression, will dictate your style.

MORE ON STYLE – THE SHORT LIST

1.   **Avoid cliches and word packages.**
Don't get pegged as a "lazy writer."

2.   **Appeal to all five senses:**
Touch
Taste
Smell
Sight
Sound

3.   **Be careful how you deal with attributions**:
He said – She said.

CHARACTERS ...

FIRST: People are characters, but not all characters are people.

SECOND: There are three character types: primary, secondary, and tertiary.

THIRD: Develop character background with the Blue Book.

FOURTH: Credible characterization depends on consistency and motivation.

FIFTH: If a reader isn't sympathetic to a character, they won't care what happens to them.

DEFINITION: In a work of fiction, people are characters – but not all characters are people.

Christine is a chararacter in Stephen King's book by that name.

What is Jabba the Hut? I don't know, but he is a character. Devils and ghosts? Frankenstein? Moby Dick, Flipper, Lassie, Donald Duck?

All of these are characters - the people and things that make your story move along.

So where do you go and what do you do when you start to populate your story? Answer: You return to that carefully detailed outline. (You'll need that outline again and again as you work your way through this process.)

THREE TYPES OF CHARACTERS

By now, you're wondering and thinking about how many characters you need, what they look like, how old they are, and what color eyes they have. The list of questions could go on forever when you're getting started on your first novel. For now though, I want you to put those questions on the back burner. Let me give you something else to stir around on the front burner.

PRIMARY: The main characters, the ones without whom your plot would come to a grinding halt.

SECONDARY: Characters who move in and out of your plot as your story progresses.

TERTIARY: Disposables, use one time and throw away.

FIRST: TERTIARY CHARACTERS...

I once saw a portfolio of characters an aspiring novelist had put together before she started her novel. The folder was full of biographical sketches and the sketches were quite complete. She had even carried her outlining to the point that she had given the characters names. I complimented her on the thoroughness of her preparation and asked some questions about one or two of the characters. "Oh, she's in a crowd scene," the woman replied. "She shouts something at my protagonist. I'll have her say something like, 'When are they going to close the gates?'"

"That's it?"

The woman nodded, "... or words to that effect."

I thumbed back through the stack of bio sketches and noted that she had gone to the trouble of giving that character a name, rank, and full-blown bio. Which is another way of saying she knew as much about that tertiary character as she did the heavyweights – protagonists and antagonists – in her story.

Why go to all that trouble? If the character only has one or two lines of dialogue, why do we need to know what she likes for breakfast, where she went to college, or why she is a Dodger fan? The bottom line here is that neither you as an author nor the reader need all that information. Learn to regard tertiary characters as disposable. The definition of a disposable character is one who is in and out of your story one time.

At this point in some of my seminars (even after reciting the above), I ask some of the attendees to describe the woman in the following scene:

99

Our hero goes to the door of an apartment in a three-story walkup. He is going to knock at the door and a woman is going to open it. The man will ask if the person he is looking for is there, and the old woman will respond she hasn't seen him.

Then I repeat my instructions: Describe that woman. You should see the pens fly. After giving them a few minutes, I ask them to read what they have written. Some describe the tattered dress the woman was wearing, how she walked with a limp, the color of her tired eyes, and maybe even something about what the hero could see in the room behind her. In most cases they write three or four, maybe more, descriptive sentences. Again I have to ask why? She doesn't need a name, an age, or anything else. All the reader needs to know is her response and the fact that it was an old woman.

Martin Cruz Smith, in his novel, *Gorky Park*, handled it this way: *"She had a scarlet slash for a mouth."* How could the reader get a better picture? Memorable? You bet. A beautiful example of tight writing by an excellent author.

Here's something that works for me in dealing with tertiary characters: If that character has no more than one or two lines of dialogue, I try to restrict myself to a one line description of that character. This is not a hard and fast rule, mind you, but it does prevent wordiness and extra bio work when I'm developing my characters.

One final word on tertiary characters: Make them unique in that brief description so that the reader will remember them and their purpose for being in your story.

SECOND: SECONDARY CHARACTERS ...

Let's start with a definition. Secondary characters make a significant contribution to your plot – but they do not carry it.

So, what do you need to tell the reader about a secondary character so that he or she can be faithfully portrayed? The answer to that question requires that you ask yourself some additional questions:

> *What do you intend to have this character do?*
> *What are the important attributes of the character?*
> *What about physical and moral strength?*
> *What about beauty or credibility?*
> *... and a whole lot more.*

The author has to come with answers to these questions so that those character dimensions can be conveyed to the reader. Also, the question of the extent to which you have to develop the character has to be balanced with how much the reader needs to know. If the reader needs more information in order to make judgments about that character, then it's up to you, the author, to provide it.

Here is the bio development guide I use for secondary characters. I try to confine my description within the context of the manuscript to one paragraph for a secondary character. I don't always succeed, but I seldom do much more than that. This example, taken from *The Prometheus Project*, introduces a character I called Sarge. My protagonist has gone to meet him for the first time.

At 6:00 the following morning, standing by the swinging doors to the Rincon's kitchen, I was approached by an

101

enormous black man with a smile highlighted by two evenly spaced gold teeth. He was wearing blood-spattered kitchen whites, a testimony to the fact that he had spent the night butchering chickens. "They say you are lookin' for me, mon," he said.

That's it, the whole introduction and description of the character I called Sarge. Later on, as the story developed, I sprinkled a few more facts on the reader about his brute strength and military background. But those were the characteristics the reader learned during Sarge's dialogue with my protagonist.

A RECOMMENDATION
Secondary characters work best for the reader when they continue to develop as the story unfolds. They achieve added dimension through the words and actions as they contribute to the story.

THIRD: PRIMARY CHARACTERS ...
Now we move into the realm of the big boppers. These are the heavyweights, the characters who will carry your story.

DEVELOPMENT
Developing major or primary characters is a totally different task. It requires meticulous recording of everything. When it comes to dealing with your primary characters, you need to know everything there is to know about them. Some of those facts may never be imparted to the reader but you need to know them so that their actions are consistent with what you have them do during the course of your novel.

When I first developed the character Thomas Carrington

Bogner for the five-book *Red* series, I started with where he was born, took him through college, flight school, his commission as a naval pilot, his marriage, the birth of his daughter, and his divorce. This process alone generated some spin-off or secondary characters such as his wife and his daughter. Both appear from time to time in several of the books in the series. At no point during this early process of giving him a background did I worry about creating a physical description. I leave that to what I call my "blue book" phase of character development.

THE BLUE BOOK OF CHARACTERS

I believe Joyce Kilmer was right: *Only God can make a tree –* or at least a good one. By the same token, I believe only God can conjure up a human being. So I don't try to compete; I use the Big Guy's guide to characters and put them in my blue book.

The blue book is nothing more than a three-ring binder in which I put the pictures of a variety of Homo sapiens that I have torn from magazines.

I am not one of my doctor's or dentist's favorite patients. Why? Because every time I see a picture in one of their magazines that I think would come in handy for my blue book, I rip it out. The same goes for when I'm getting the oil changed, waiting for a prescription, or getting a haircut – I rip. I look for pictures of old women, young women, middle-aged women, women with glasses, with children, and beautiful women. (Don't waste your time trying to find a picture of an ugly woman – impossible; they don't allow their picture to be taken.) I look for pictures of women at work, at play, being wives, being lovers, and being mothers. I conduct the same

103

search for men and children. Then I place all of them in clear view plastic sheets and put them in my three-ring book.

Why do I do this? Because it is an enormous time saver. When I want to create a character, I simply thumb through my blue book until I find a picture that coincides with that image in my mind's eye. Everything is there, all the lines in the face, the cut of the hair, the set of the jaw. I don't have to make it up; it's there and it's believable because that person really exists. It's even more effective when you select pictures in color. That saves you from having to remember whether your character has brown or blond hair, blue or green eyes, white or tobacco-stained teeth. When I have that much to get me started, the rest is a piece of cake. I make characters as tall, as broad, as muscular, or as anything as I want them to be.

Drumming up characters for my story then becomes a casting call. I thumb through the blue book until I find a picture of someone who looks like a Russian general or an Iraqi terrorist and go from there. After I know what the character looks like, I go about the process of giving that character a background and characteristics – but again, only as much as the reader will need to know to make them believable.

A story or two about how this blue book has worked for me may help.

MY EXPERIENCE: *RED TIDE* ...

When I began putting the story board together for *Red Tide*, I was faced with the daunting task of developing no less than 13 Russian generals and KGB agents, in addition to several Jamaicans and a fist full of Americans, military and otherwise. I found the pictures I needed for the Russians in several back issues of *Forbes* magazine. There they were, all pictures of major U.S. corporate executives: dour, scowling, and looking as if they had indigestion. Do I need to tell you they looked exactly the way I envisioned Russian generals? I cut them out, gave them Russian names, and sprinted through my outline.

DEVELOPMENT OF T.C. BOGNER ...

My second story along this line has to do with developing the character of then-Commander T.C. Bogner for my *Red* series. (I say "then" because he has since been promoted.) It took me several weeks to find the image I was looking for. I found it in an issue of *Fortune* and since that time I have kept his picture in a spot where I can clearly see it. After five books, I like to think I know everything there is to know about my protagonist, but my readers don't. I have never given a complete physical description of Bogner in any one *Red* book. At book signings I have had a number of different readers tell me what they think he looks like, but so far no one has really put all the elements together. To my readers, Bogner looks like whatever the reader imagines him to look like. I like that. It personalizes him for each reader.

PITFALL

There is one more caution I feel I need to make about this blue book method of casting your novel: Don't fall into the easy trap of collecting only pictures of pretty people. Hey, look around, there are some very homely dudes out there, and you do want your characters to be realistic, don't you?

When you think about casting your story, remember

what people really look like. In real life, some folks wear glasses, some are fat, some are skinny, and some are homely. Men wear mustaches, beards, have warts, double chins, crooked teeth, and are not always clean-shaven. Some women wear lots of make-up and some wear none at all. They may wear hats or jeans, dresses, heels, or none of the above. There is long hair, short hair, and no hair.

Get the drift? Capture the essence of the human condition. Keep these factors in mind when you start designing even your primary characters.

FLESHING OUT YOUR PRIMARY CHARACTERS

Okay? Now we're making some progress. We have our primary characters identified physically, we know what roles we want them to play in our drama, and we have pictures of them in our little blue book. That is a good start. But now we have to flesh them out. To do this, we have to deal with two very important aspects of developing a character:
1.   Credibility
2.   Characterization

CREDIBILITY ...

Credible characterization depends on two things: consistency and motivation. We'll take a look at consistency first.

FIRST: CONSISTENCY...

Whenever you portray a character's reaction to another character or a situation developing in your plot, you have to consider several questions. Ask yourself:

1. Is this behavior or response consistent with the character as I have presented and portrayed him or her in the story up to this point?

2. Is this the way my character would talk, think, and react under the circumstances in this particular plot situation?

3. Is there a change in the way the character is reacting? If there is, have I made it clear to the reader why this change in character behavior is happening?

A RECOMMENDATION

Does this sound like I'm getting picky all of a sudden? Is that a change in my behavior? Perhaps, perhaps not. I could assure you that I am only stressing an important point:

Having your character suddenly altering their behavior or no apparent reason will cause your readers to wonder both about you as an author and the way they had the character pegged.

On the other hand, if your character is a raving

schizophrenic, you don't have to give reasons
why that person's behavior has suddenly
changed. If there is some kind of epiphany
event taking place in your story, make certain
the reader knows it.

SECOND: CHARACTERIZATION...
1.   Motivation …

What motivates your character to do what he or she
does? You know, but does the reader? What made Quint, the
skipper of the *Orca* in *Jaws*, be willing to put his life on the line
to kill the shark? We learned – fairly late in the story – that he
had been a member of the crew of the *Indianapolis* when it
delivered the atomic bomb at the end of WWII. Quint
described how the *Indianapolis* was sunk and over a thousand
men were lost to the sharks in a subsequent feeding frenzy. The
motivation is suddenly clear; Quint is actually killing all sharks
when he goes after the rogue shark in the book. Motivation
understood? You bet. But not until the author explained the
what and *why* of Quint's actions.

PITFALL
The caution here is to make certain the reader
knows why something is happening with a
particular character. Often the reason is apparent.
But many times it isn't. On the other hand, if
you're writing a mystery, maybe you don't want
the reader to know just yet. As an author, you have
to avoid cut-out doll characters and characters that
lack motivation and credibility.

2. Names and apparel ...

Most authors I know have their own way of naming their characters. There is the phone book method, the tombstone method, the obituary method, the sports page method, and several others. When I'm populating a novel, I often use a phone book for the names of characters other than my protagonist(s) and antagonist(s). First, I select last names. Then, I go through and randomly select first names so that I haven't intentionally identified a real person.

I consciously try to capture some Spanish, Greek, Irish, Italian, and other ethnic names, just to make certain I have a mix that sounds like a real group of people.

PITFALL

One thing you do want to watch is the tendency to use too many *cute* or *buzz* names like Bambi, Gidget or Barbie. These names tend to become outdated and when your novel is reprinted – for the fifth time – years from now, you want it to still sound somewhat contemporary.

3. Dressing your character ...

This is probably as good a place as any to mention this: As a rule, men do not know how to dress women characters – and women don't always – would you believe, seldom? – know how to dress men. Women only know how they *wish* men would dress. I saw a manuscript not long ago where a young woman had her protagonist in a romance novel going off to his blue-collar job (construction crew) in Jordach jeans and a Calvin Klein shirt. Get real.

As for you men, you may as well admit it; you have no

idea what women consider appropriate attire for an occasion. And even if you did, you wouldn't know what half the garments in a woman's wardrobe are even called. Get help.

A RECOMMENDATION
Get a Sears catalog and keep it close by your word processor. That way you can look up a model who is dressed reasonably close to the way you envision your heroine or hero looking.

Depending on the kind of story you are working on, you may need a catalog from Frederick's of Hollywood, or, in upscale cases, a GQ or a Vogue catalog close by as well.

SEVEN THINGS TO REMEMBER WHEN YOU ARE CREATING CHARACTERS

1. **Make your reader love or hate your primary characters.**
   Be certain the reader knows the character is important. You must make each one distinguishable, memorable, and remarkable. Above all, make each one credible and consistent. Introduce one primary character at a time.

2. **Get *real* when you create your primary characters.**
   If your character is too good to be true, he won't be real and neither will she. Even your primary characters should be somewhat flawed.

3. **Introduce your primary characters early in your story.**
    Rule of thumb – somewhere in the first chapter.

4. **Don't rely on physical descriptions only.**
    Get your reader inside the head of primary characters and make them multi-dimensional.

5. **Flesh out your primary characters.**
    Even good people hesitate and vacillate on occasion.

6. **Make your hero a HERO.**
    Your reader has an emotional investment in your protagonist. Let her win. Write your dark novel later.

7. **Study real people.**
    Add a little writer's imagination, sprinkle it with responsible author's license, and start developing your characters.

THE NEED TO CREATE SYMPATHETIC CHARACTERS

FACT: **If a reader isn't sympathetic to a character, they won't care what happens to them.**

Let me rephrase that factoid to read: The more your reader can identify with your characters, the more likely they are to care – have sympathy – for them.

EXAMPLE: Suppose you pick up the morning paper and read that 300 people died in a typhoon in China. How do you feel? Many readers will look at the news philosophically and somewhat detached. Three hundred out of a nation populated with more than 1.4 billion people is a very small percentage. An equally small proportion of the American population is likely to have an emotional investment in people in a country so far away. Psychologists will even tell you there is a thread of "I'm glad it didn't happen here" and "I'm glad it wasn't anyone I know" kind of thinking going on in the reader's mind.

Now, scale down your thinking and imagine an earthquake in California. It killed 40 people. Suddenly the event is a little more intimate. Why? It's closer to home, right here in the United States. This is where proximity as well as sympathy also becomes a critical element in creating a character. You may know people, even have family in California. Your concern is clearly elevated.

Scale it down even further. You read that a girl, age six, has been kidnapped right here in your hometown. You don't know the child, but you are far more likely to be upset than you were over either of the earlier events I described. If you have children, especially one that age, you are likely to feel real distress. (Proximity factor at work.)

Even without physical details like the color of the child's eyes, hair color, height, weight, where she went to school, or the fact that she was looking for her lost dog when she disappeared, you feel much closer to this situation.

This is a lesson for you new writers: You can make the connection between your readers and your characters in a few carefully chosen words. Writers call that *reader sympathy*. Keep that term in mind whenever you are populating a novel.

Reader sympathy develops when the reader can identify with your character. If your reader doesn't have sympathy for that character, they won't give a hoot and a holler what happens to that character. If they don't care, in all probability, you've just lost them.

A RECOMMENDATION
You don't have to paint a complete biographical sketch of each character in your story. Your job is to make each character memorable, important and necessary to your story line.

CHARACTERS – THE SHORT LIST

1.   Not all characters are people – Lassie and Jabba the Hut.

2.   Characters come in three types: tertiary, secondary, primary.

3.   Create a Blue Book for character development.

4.   Credibility comes from consistency and motivation.

5.   Seven things to remember when creating characters:

   a.   A reader should love your hero and hate your villain.
   b.   Make the characters *real*.
   c.   Introduce primary characters early.
   d.   Don't rely on physical description only.
   e.   Flesh out primary characters.
   f.   Make your hero a HERO.
   g.   Study real people.

13

DIALOGUE ...

FIRST: **Be aware and record for the reader the total environment.**

SECOND: **Nonverbal responses are important for conveying subtleties of meaning.**

THIRD: **Write tight dialogue.**

FOURTH: **Awkward, unrealistic dialogue is a sign of an amateur writer.**

    I've saved the toughest for last, which is another way of saying that I believe the most difficult component of good commercial fiction to master is dialogue. Why? Because most folks approaching their first novel do not have a solid concept of dialogue. If I were to ask ten aspiring writers to define dialogue, their answers would sound something like "conversation between characters in a work of fiction" or "an exchange of ideas and words between characters."

    Not bad, and to some extent those definitions work. But to a writer of commercial fiction, that isn't quite enough. So what is enough?

CALISTHENICS

Let me show you. Haul out that voice recorder
you keep handy – you followed that suggestion,
didn't you? – and crank up your VCR. We're
going to take an in-depth look at writing dialogue.

SELECT A FAVORITE MOVIE.

For the purposes of this little demonstration, I'll use
Jaws again. (I use either *Jaws* or *Casablanca* in my seminars.)

PLAY A SCENE INVOLVING DIALOGUE.

I will refer to the scene from *Jaws* where Quint, Hooper,
and Brody are sitting down in the galley of the *Orca* after their
first encounter with the shark. It is night. Hooper and Quint
have had several beers, Brody is standing apart from them, but
there is extended dialogue between all three characters. The
object here is for you to play that scene up to and through the
point where Quint reveals he was on the *Indianapolis*. Your
job is to record the dialogue only. Ignore everything else.

REPLAY THE SCENE.

This time **listen to the other sounds**. The grunts, the
laughter, the distant sound of a buoy, setting the beer bottle
down hard on the table, etc.

REPLAY THE SCENE AGAIN.

This time **mute the soundtrack.** As you watch, **make
careful note of expressions and gestures.** There are several
touch gestures – Quint pushing his hat up to show the scars,
pushing his sleeve up to show where he encountered a shark –
and some of the same for Hooper. Make note of taste or smell

sensations and ask what do those characters hear? The scene concludes when they hear a loud thumping sound – the sound of the shark ramming into the hull of the *Orca*.

REWRITE YOUR SCENE.

Now, take a scene from your present novel and write a passage of dialogue that reflects all of the kinds of sensory input you have just experienced in the scene from *Jaws*.

Ask yourself, what did I experience, not just hear, when those actors were talking?

MEANINGFUL DIALOGUE

Dialogue consists of much more than just words.
When we really listen, we also do a lot of seeing, and we turn on our mental recorders.

We recorded the effect of props in *Jaws*...
1.   The swinging lamp over the table.
2.   The sound of the buoy in the distance.
3.   The characters shifting in the seats.

In other words, your job is to be aware, and record, for the reader, where appropriate, the total environment where the exchange took place.

A RECOMMENDATION

If the dialogue you record for your readers takes place in a social or all verbal vacuum, you have missed a real opportunity to enrich your novel by showing, as well as recording, what happened.

NONVERBAL DIALOGUE

Think about:

1. What does a shrug of the shoulders mean? Indifference? Lack of knowledge? Who cares?
2. What does the nod of the head mean? I hear you? I agree with you? Proceed?
3. What does the shake of the head mean? No? I disagree?
4. What does drumming the fingers on the table mean? Impatience? Boredom?

Nonverbal responses are an important tool for conveying the subtleties of meaning in dialogue. Remember that not all human beings are able or inclined to articulate how they feel. If you have a true cross-section of characters in your dialogue, somewhere in your story there are bound to be individuals who are reticent. Nonverbal responses, such as stamping the foot, sighing, yawning, shaking the head, averting the eyes, or staring off into the distance can be effective in dialogue.

DEFINITION OF DIALOGUE

Dialogue is any exchange between characters in a work of fiction that you, the author, want the reader to experience.

That means that when you create a scene in which two or more characters communicate, it is your responsibility to deal with all aspects of that exchange: the setting (a room, a cattle drive, a space ship), the body language (shifting in the chair, tapping on the table, twisting in the saddle), and the facial expressions (scowls, smiles, frowns, even empty stares).

"SNAPPY DIALOGUE ALONE CAN CONVEY FEELINGS"

There are times when narrative is not necessary to support dialogue. Take this example from my book, *The Prometheus Project*. My protagonist, Elliott Wages, is talking to his mentor, Cosmo Leach, in a diner.

"Elliott, let me assure you it's not our government. Someone else is calling the shots."
"Who?"
"Are you saying you are interested?"
"Dammit, Cosmo, I got up at four o'clock this morning, plowed my way through six inches of snow, caught the local 'fly and die' into O'Hare, flew down here – and you ask if I'm interested? Hell, yes, I'm interested. You called, I came; that's the way it works with friends."
"Suppose I told you that Schuster Laboratories had an interest in all of this."

What you have just read is simple, straightforward dialogue between two men. (Note: No attributions in this tightly written scene.) The purpose of this whole scene was to convey information to the reader by having a secondary character, Cosmo Leach, inform the protagonist, Elliott Wages, about a critical element of the plot. It was an exchange that did not require any other kind of support.

Got it? All right, now compare the above to the following where the dialogue is designed to create a total experience for the reader.

NARRATIVE WOVEN INTO THE DIALOGUE

In this scene, Elliott and Cosmo have gone to meet Bearing Schuster, an aging drug baron, at his estate overlooking the Gulf of Mexico. Cosmo is speaking.

"Bearing, this is the young man I was telling you about."

The old man studied him for a moment. "Youth is a relative thing," Schuster wheezed. At the same time he was turning his face back toward the gulf. "How old are you, Mr. Wages?"

"Mentally, spiritually, or physically?"

The moment Wages said it, Bearing's eyes darted back toward him. This time his stare was less indifferent. A slight, sardonic smile indicated he was amused by Elliott's answer. "Do you like the view, Mr. Wages?"

"The blonde or the gulf?"

Here now is a scene where more than direct dialogue comes into play. Bearing Schuster betrays his preoccupation with the view or his boredom with the situation by simply turning away from Elliott. This is clearly nonverbal dialogue. The verb *wheezed* conveys not only how the line was delivered but also perhaps something about the old man's health.

Then the reader sees how Schuster's mood changes because he likes Elliott's irreverent answer. The sardonic smile gives the reader all the information the reader needs to draw some conclusions about Bearing Schuster. Some may like him. Others won't.

WRITE TIGHT DIALOGUE

If you have written tight dialogue, the reader experiences the whole scene and the reader's level of awareness can be increased about other aspects of the story or other dimensions of the character delivering the lines.

FACT: When you have written tight dialogue, the reader actually reads it as though he or she is looking from one character to the other.

Dialogue, like every other aspect of writing commercial fiction that sells, takes practice – a great deal of practice. Don't be surprised if you spend more time writing, re-writing, and editing the dialogue portions of your story than any other element of your novel.

Let's move on. What we've discussed about this topic so far constitutes little more than an overview of dialogue.

GUIDELINES

FIRST: USE DIALECTS SPARINGLY

In most sections of the country, people have dialects. Where I come from, it is not unusual to hear someone say, "Did cha eat chet?" Translation: "Did you eat yet?" It may not be grammatically correct, but that's the way we talk back home. So, if I wrote, "Have you had anything to eat yet?" it would sound strange to the folks I grew up with.

When I feel I must use dialects, I try to write dialogue as it sounds. But I keep it to a minimum, giving only a hint of dialect, then leaving the rest of the interpretation to the reader.

121

A RECOMMENDATION

Minimize dialect in dialogue. In conversations between two people from the same region, elevate one character's dialect. In other words, use the contractions that signify local dialect and contrast those with the other character's somewhat cleaned-up, less pronounced, version. In that way you have cut the use of heavy dialect in two and eliminated at least half of your problem. Study the following example in which two characters from my book, *The Pond*, are talking:

"I tole 'em to bring the body back here when they was done withit."
"Back here? What did you do that fer?"
"Cause the sheriff tole me ta do it."
"You damn fool. Sheriff Clayborn don't even know we found the damn gun. He could be in onit."

In small doses, something like the above works.

PITFALL

But consider this: A New York-based copy editor may be reading your manuscript and that editor may or may not understand what you are trying to achieve. In fact, she may well think you're a real dumbo who doesn't know how to spell. Add to this the fact that some readers find dialect very hard to swallow.

EXAMPLE: Years ago I had several occasions to make telephone calls to an engineering firm in Dallas. A charming woman who had been raised in Barker, Louisiana, answered their phone. Her standard greeting was an enthusiastic "Hahhhh" (however you spell it). If you, as an author, were able to capture that greeting and use it in your story, your dialogue would contain a hefty slice of realism and accurately convey a heavy regional dialect. The operative word in that above sentence is if. Actually, there are several ifs involved: if you can capture it, if the editor buys it, and if the reader understands it.

The question then becomes: "How do you know if your attempts to write dialect in dialogue are working?" Reach for that tape recorder again and read the passage into your machine. Then, if you can follow what is being said with your eyes closed, the dialogue — with dialect — is probably working. But that still doesn't mean an editor will buy it. The editor may not have a voice recorder or the patience to help a new writer work through the problem of dialect. (Read that: **REJECTION.**)

SECOND: USING CONTRACTIONS

Rule of thumb: You **can use** contractions **in dialogue**, but **not narrative.** I use contractions in dialogue only when I feel it would be clumsy not to, or if I feel I would not be portraying my character accurately to do anything else.

Be aware. Whether the contractions are actually there or not, some folks will read exactly what they want to *hear* when they are reading your masterpiece of carefully constructed dialogue. I once listened to my sister-in-law read something I had written. I didn't even recognize it as my work.

THIRD: WRITING ACTION INTO YOUR DIALOGUE PASSAGES

1. **Character movements:** In the course of conversation – characters may shift positions, scratch their noses, close their eyes, look bored, interrupt, sigh, roll their eyes, take a sip of their drinks, gesture, maybe even light cigarettes.
2. **Character's foibles:** Another thing, some people don't complete what they start to say. Often they wander about using indirection and free association to guide the conversation.
3. **Essential elements:** As an author, you should record only those essential elements that will affect the reader's interpretation of the dialogue. What are those essentials? Well, just about anything that makes the scene complete. Maybe you describe the clutter in the room or reveal the gunman's nervousness. Work in anything that enriches the scene, fleshes out the character, or reveals something about the character's behavior.

CALISTHENICS

ONE: Let's apply what we have just learned. Write a scene involving the following: Two people on a bed, male and female. They scratch their noses, wet their lips, and so on. Write a revealing scene. Invent dialogue. Use any or all –dream up your own – of the above actions. One-half page.

How did you do?

TWO: Let's try another one. Two gunslingers.
A dusty corral. Maybe you don't have them say
very much, but there is a great deal of nonverbal
dialogue in a scene like this. It's up to you to
capture it: flinching, scowling, twitching, nervousness,
and only an occasional verbal exchange.

Finished? A bit tougher? Probably. We writing
types have a tendency to fall back on dialogue in
situations where we have had little experience with
a similar event.

FOURTH: DIFFERENT CHARACTERS DELIVER THEIR LINES IN DIFFERENT WAYS

Showing *how* a line is delivered enables the reader to
pick up on the mood of the character without the author having
to describe it. All of the following are responses to a previous
line of dialogue.

"Why?" Patty whimpered. (verbal)

Luke clenched his fists. (nonverbal)

Candy bit her lip. (nonverbal)

Arlo laughed. (semi-verbal)

In each of these cases you get something extra in the
response: An indication of the character's mood, insight into
the character's apprehension, disdain – or was it mirth? You
could write, *Toby said, "No."* Or you could write, *Toby shook
his head.* You could break up several lines of dialogue by using
the second version and show some action.

As Dr. Wendell Mayo put it in one of my graduate
classes years ago, "... **ventilate the text or suffocate your
reader**." (Good advice.)

CALISTHENICS

Now, take those two scenes you just wrote and haul out that voice recorder. Read your carefully drafted scene and dialogue into the machine. If the action helps the scene, stay with it. If it doesn't, dump it. Some dialogue exchanges are far snappier without action.

FIFTH: REALISTIC LANGUAGE – DEALING WITH PROFANITY

A psychologist friend of mine once told me that 9 out of 10 people use some form of profanity. But their usage hinges on their definition of what is profane and what isn't. Trust me, there is no profane word that hasn't been written, and most readers of commercial fiction have read them. But here I have to point out an important distinction.

THE DIFFERENCE BETWEEN PROFANITY AND OBSCENITY

Let me define each as a writer sees it. **Profanity is** the damns, the hells, and so on (common to most people) and many, many exchanges of conversation in the real world.

Obscenities, on the other hand, are the words you don't want your mother or your children to know you know. You and you alone are going to have to make the distinction about which words fall into which category.

IT'S YOUR CHOICE

One friend of mine writes mysteries absent of profanity. Another, also a mystery writer, uses language that would make Jackie Collins blush. Profanity and obscenities are an element of writing you need to think about. Sooner or later, you are going to develop an unsavory character that blurts out things you didn't know you were capable of putting on paper. Think about how you are going to handle profanity and obscenities now, before you write yourself into a corner. If you end up writing a line of dialogue for a 250-pound teamster like, "Oh, darn," when a forklift runs over his foot, some editor will laugh you all the way to the *return to sender* pile.

A RECOMMENDATION
Study your market to see how other writers in your genre handle profanity and obscenity.

SIXTH: IN DIALOGUE, CHARACTERS DO NOT ALWAYS RESPOND TO QUESTIONS
Look at the following example:

"Damn it, Bert, I think we can make it. What do you think?"
Bert hesitated.
"Well," Sam insisted, "...what do you think?"

Simple dialogue. Ask yourself, does the nonverbal response make the passage more or less effective? Bert could have said, "No." He could have said, "Maybe." He could have said lots of things. **You**, as an author, **have to decide if a verbal response would have sounded contrived, shallow, maybe even stilted.**

The point is that there are times when a non-response can be more effective than a counter response. You decide when.

A RECOMMENDATION

Break up a long sequence of line after line of give-and-take dialogue with some small action or nonverbal response.

Want some examples of small actions? I find relatively insignificant actions, such as those that follow, useful when I want to ventilate my dialogue passages.

He paused to load his pipe.
She walked to the window and stared out.
She worried the corners of her handkerchief.
Beth hesitated, still weighing her words.
Sam rubbed his chin, waiting.

FINAL WORD: PRACTICE WRITING DIALOGUE UNTIL YOU MASTER IT

No single element of your writing reveals the extent of your professionalism like the dialogue you write.

Nothing is as important when you are trying to tell a great story.

Good dialogue breathes life into your story by lending immediacy and action to it.

1. You can pace a scene at breakneck speed by writing rapid-fire exchanges between characters.
2. You can draw a reader into your novel by creating a sense of eavesdropping, maybe even a sense of participation.
3. Great dialogue can even overcome some of your other writing weaknesses.

Awkward, unrealistic dialogue is another sign of an amateur writer. So work on this aspect endlessly until your manuscript sings.

CALISTHENICS

In an earlier chapter of this handbook, I asked you to write a 250-word synopsis of the story you either intend to write or the one you have already started. Then, in a subsequent chapter I asked you to find a way to reduce that 250-word synopsis to 125 words. Both are good practice when it comes to learning to write tight – getting the garbage – the non-essentials – out of your writing.

Now we take this exercise a step further. Reduce those 125 words to 25 words. Don't groan. You can do it. If you haven't done the two drills up to this point, do them now. Why? Because you're going to need those 25 tightly written words when you get ready to prepare that all-important *submission* package. You do want to sell your epic, don't you?

And just to prove it can be done: *Little Red Riding Hood* is a story about a girl who disobeys her mother and is almost eaten by a wolf before being miraculously rescued. (25 words)

DIALOGUE — THE SHORT LIST

1. **Dialogue is any exchange between characters** in a work of fiction that you, the author, want the reader to experience.

2. **Dialogue reflects all kinds of sensory input.** Learn and use the VCR dialogue calisthenic. Then, ask yourself, what did I experience, not just hear, when those actors were talking?

3. **Sometimes dialogue is nonverbal.**

4. **Remember the 6 Dialogue Guidelines:**
   a. Use **dialects sparingly.**
   b. **Feel free to use contractions** in dialogue.
   c. **Write action into your dialogue.**
   d. Remember **different characters speak in different voices.**
   e. Keep your language **realistic.**
   f. In dialogue sometimes **a non-response can be more effective than a counter response.**

AGENTS ...

FIRST: Editors rely on agents to send them only publishable, professional material.

SECOND: Avoid an agent who charges you a reading fee.

THIRD: A proposal attempts to sell nonfiction; while a synopsis attempts to sell fiction.

FOURTH: When dealing with an agent, be yourself – but act professional.

FACTS ABOUT AGENTS

QUESTIONS IN WRITING SEMINARS

If someone were to ask me to list the most frequently asked questions in one of my writing seminars, one of them would certainly be:

Q. Should I get an agent before I write my novel, or should I wait until after I have sold one and then look for an agent?

A. Write the novel. Then worry about literary agents.

FACTS ABOUT AGENTS: MAKING MONEY...

Literary agents make money when they sell a literary property – your novel, for example. Editors, even more so since publishers have gotten on the downsizing kick, rely on agents to send them only publishable, professional material. In this sense, while the agent is representing your work, the agent is also putting his or her own reputation on the line by making a value judgment about the work. In effect, your agent is telling that editor, "I know the kind of work you buy, I know what you're looking for, and I know the degree of excellence you demand in manuscripts. I've taken all these factors into consideration and believe this work meets your requirements."

Q.   Are you telling me an agent might *not* send my work to a publisher?

A.   Yes. To an agent, your work is business. If it isn't up to a publisher's standards, the agent won't submit it.

FACTS ABOUT AGENTS: BUSINESS RELATIONSHIPS ...

An agent that sends an editor a manuscript that is below par is jeopardizing a business relationship with that editor. So you can understand why a good agent is reluctant to take on new writers until they have proven they can do what they say they will do. Agents know all too well how many beginners start manuscripts and how few of those manuscripts are finished.

Q.   How will I know if my work is commercial?

A.   Your agent knows.

FACTS ABOUT AGENTS: CHANGES ...

Your agent serves another purpose in the publishing

132

cycle. A good agent will read, assess, and often recommend changes in a manuscript before submitting it to a publisher. Mine does. When I send a manuscript to New York, my agent gives it a thorough read and discusses with me changes he believes the story needs to make it more saleable. It all goes back to whether your agent believes you have written a book that folks will be eager to purchase.

Q.   How can I judge my agent's performance?
A.   The same way you judge any professional.

FACTS ABOUT AGENT: EFFECTIVENESS ...

A touch of reality here: Not all agents are effective. In my first life, 25 years in industry, I worked with manufacturer's agents. The principle is the same as in publishing; only the product is different.

I learned then that there are as many different performance levels with agents as there are with any other professionals.

1.   Some agents work hard, others don't.
2.   Some agents handle only two or three major authors, and some have a whole stable of authors.
3.   I talked to one agency – three agents – that represented 153 authors. Are you going to get better representation from someone who handles only three authors – or one that represents several?

FACTS ABOUT AGENTS: SITUATIONS VARY ...

A literary agent that may be perfect for me may not be right for you. You'll have to shop around after your submission package is ready to market. But that shouldn't be such a daunting task; after all, you had to find the right tax man, the right doctor, the right lawyer, etc.

PITFALL

I would be remiss if I didn't say this: If there
is anything to avoid, it is an agent who charges
you a fee to read your work before he or she
agrees to represent you. Legitimate agents
don't earn their living as book doctors or
professional readers.

The one point I can't stress enough is that as
a first time author, you must have something
to show an agent. There is nothing better than
a well-written, polished, finished novel.

Q. **How do I write a proposal to sell my first novel?**
A. **First, let's get the lingo right. You write a *proposal*
to sell nonfiction. You write a *synopsis* to sell a work
of fiction.**

PITFALL

As a beginning author, it is highly unlikely (read
that, damn near impossible) to sell your first novel
on the basis of a synopsis.

Why? Because the publishing industry doesn't
know you. They have no guarantee that you
will ever finish the novel. (Repeat: Don't go
agent hunting until you can hand them something
they can evaluate, like a finished manuscript.)
What are you going to do, show an agent a stack
of blank pages and assure them that someday
there will be a novel written on that paper? The
world, particularly the publishing world, doesn't
work that way.

Q.   I hear that I can't get an agent until I'm published, and I can't get published without an agent. So, what do I do?

A.   For starters, stop worrying.

RECOMMENDATION

Trust me, if you have written a novel worthy of publication, this problem goes away. If you are still having anxiety attacks, buy a copy of Jeff Herman's excellent *Writer's Guide to Book Editors, Publishers, and Literary Agents*. Pick out some agencies that handle the kind of fiction you write. Find out how many new writers they decided to represent the previous year. If they offer free information about their agency, send for it. The information will probably tell you how to make a submission. When you know that, you'll know how to look like a real professional when you do submit your manuscript.

Q.   What's the best way to deal with an agent?

A.   Be yourself – but act professional.

FACTS ABOUT AGENTS: PROFESSIONALISM ...

I asked my agent what his number one objection was to working with new writers. His answer was, "*Their lack of professionalism.*" He then went on to recite the blunders he associates with new writers:

"*They take up too much time on the telephone. They ramble on, wasting time with small talk, looking for positive reinforcement about their writing, hoping to say something that*

135

*will make me give extra attention to their work. Hell, when I'm
in my office, I'm on the telephone working the publishers for
my authors. I have a window of about four hours each work
day when editors are willing to accept calls. I can't be wasting
precious time holding someone's hand."*

Q.   What if my book doesn't sell?
A.   If you want to become an author, write another one.

HOW TO APPROACH AN AGENT
PLAN A: ACCEPTANCE ...
        Let's say your novel is finished and you have identified
two or more literary agencies that you believe are the kind of
agencies that you want to represent you. You could...
1.   Call the agency and verify the name of an individual in
        that agency to whom you want to send your manuscript,
        confirm that he or she is still with the agency, and check
        to see whether that agency accepts work from
        unpublished writers. If you are fortunate enough to get
        an affirmative response, find out what he or she wants
        to see in a submission package. Thank the person on
        the other end of the line and hang up. Don't chitchat.
        Don't try to pre-sell your book. Be professional.

2.   Prepare a professional submission package that includes
        a query letter, a resume of your writing experience and a
        synopsis, or whatever the agent requested. Some
        agencies will request sample chapters as well as a
        synopsis.

3.   Send the package promptly (read that, immediately) and
        give the agency at least 10 days before you make your
        second call. In that call, all you do is verify that the

136

agent received your package. Do not ask what they think of it. In all probability it will be a couple of weeks, or longer, before they get around to reading it. I can assure you, if your manuscript sings, they will get back to you. If not, they will tell you why they are not interested.

MY EXPERIENCE: No interest by this agency ...

While I was writing this handbook, I received a call from a friend of mine who had just been informed by an agency that it was not interested in representing his book. I had to assure him that did not mean the agency did not like his writing. An agency's, or agent's, refusal to handle your manuscript may mean nothing more than the agency is already representing a similar work or an author with a similar style. It could mean the subject matter is not currently a hot market, or any of a hundred other valid reasons. Remember that a rejection is an expression of *"no interest by this agency."* That's all it means. It is no indication another agency won't leap at the chance to represent your book.

PLAN 2A: REJECTION ...

If you've been rejected, go to the second agency on your list and try again. The "T" in the word writer stands for *tenacity.*

1.   Let's say the third agency on your list wants to see the whole manuscript. Send a *clean* copy and take some patience pills. It will likely be six, eight, perhaps more weeks before you hear anything. Agents have to read manuscripts and figure out where they can best be marketed. Reading manuscripts takes time, and if this is a full-blown, market-driven, successful literary agency,

the agents are busy. Believe me, the writers who are already clients of that agency want it that way; that means they are selling books and making money.

2.   If you haven't heard anything after 10 weeks, call the agency. Again, be brief and be professional. If they say they aren't interested, don't whimper and ask why. In all likelihood, they will tell you. At least it will give you something to consider before you try again.

3.   If you are rejected several times in succession, you should probably start questioning the market appeal of your work or the quality of your writing. Re-read your novel. Re-think your story. Re-plan your market strategy.

4.   Finally, keep this in mind. Agents make money when they sell books. They need a product to sell. Regardless of what you have heard, agents are looking for new writers who can meet the demands (great story, great writing) of the market place. Above all, do not get discouraged.

PLAN B: WRITING CONFERENCES ...

Several aspiring novelists I know have tucked their manuscripts under their arm and hustled off to a writer's conference because the conference committee had invited agents for the specific purpose of meeting new authors. If you are convinced you have a work that would sell if only you could get it in front of the right person, this is a plan that could be worth trying.

In this case, the chances are excellent that you can

arrange to have a face-to-face with a real, live agent. Granted, it will probably be a brief encounter. At the Midwest Writers Conference held annually in Muncie, Indiana, pre-registered writers are usually given a thirty-minute interview. Another approach that I've seen at several conferences is the group interview in which the agent asks you to tell about your novel. (This is where that 25-word synopsis you struggled with and didn't think you could write, comes in.) If the agent believes your plot sounds interesting and marketable, you will probably be invited back for a more in-depth session. You've really connected if the agent then says, "I'd like to see the complete work."

A RECOMMENDATION

Deal with agents one at a time. Do not make multiple inquiries to agents. You could end up paying both agents if the book sells. Or worse, and even more expensive, end up in litigation. Don't send a copy of a manuscript to a publisher and an agent at the same time. If you want an agency to represent you, let the agency decide where your manuscript should go. Be professional.

AGENTS — THE SHORT LIST

1.   **Write your novel** before you worry about getting an agent.

2.   Sending **your manuscript** to an editor **puts the agent's reputation on the line**, as well as yours.

3.   **Proposals** sell **non-fiction books**; **novels** require a **synopsis**.

4.   **Be yourself; act professional** if you want to impress an agent.

5.   Deal with **agents one at a time**.

6.   **Avoid agents** who charge a **reading fee**.

PUBLISHERS

FIRST: **Submission to a publisher is much the same as for an agent.**

SECOND: **Direct submissions end up in the *slush* pile.**

THIRD: **If you want to be a professional anything, it takes tons of work.**

      Nowhere is it written you have to sell your novel through an agent. You can, if you wish, go straight to a publisher with your first book.

SUBMITTING YOUR NOVEL TO A PUBLISHER:
The steps are almost the same as submitting your work to an agent.
1.   You do the same research – searching out the names of publishers who publish the kind of novel you have written, and you do it from the same sources mentioned earlier.
2.   You call, verify if a particular editor is still with the publishing company, and go through the same steps you would have gone through if you were submitting your work to an agent.

PITFALL
Anything else – direct submissions without
the literary foreplay – and you, my aspiring
novelist friend, are doomed to end up in the
dreaded slush pile.

THE *SLUSH* PILE

The slush pile is just what it sounds like: a pile of
unsolicited manuscripts. If there is a long-shot way of selling
your novel, this is it. To have your novel plucked from the
slush pile and even read is a major miracle. One writer I know
compares it to building a swimming pool and waiting for one of
those infamous 100-year rains to fill it.

But if you are the kind who goes to the racetrack and
plays long shots, why not try it? Cost involved should total no
more than $40 or $50 to cover copies, postage, SASE, etc. Be
prepared to wait three months or more for any kind of answer.
Even then, don't be surprised if your copy of the manuscript
looks as though no one has even looked at it. It probably hasn't
been, especially if it was unsolicited.

However, it can happen.

MY EXPERIENCE: *Black Death* ...

My first published novel, *Black Death*, was plucked
from a slush pile and sent to a homemaker in New Jersey for a
first reading. She liked it, gave it to an editorial assistant, and it
eventually passed through the hands of several editors before an
offer was extended. Rare? You bet. I later learned it was the
first novel they had purchased out of their slush pile in several
years.

DISCOURAGED?

Don't be. If you wanted to be a professional golfer, it would take just as much time and practice. Perhaps more. If you want to be a professional anything, it takes tons of work. Like all professions, no matter how much blood, sweat, and tears you put into it, there is always the chance you won't make it. But if you really want – I mean *really, really want* to be an author, you'll keep trying. If you do make it, the rewards (psychological, lifestyle, and often financial) are fantastic.

Let me repeat a story I told earlier – because it is worth repeating:

At the conclusion of a recent writer's conference, I heard an attendee say that she had "*had it*." She pointed out that she had been writing for five years and she was no closer to being published than when she started. That's too bad, but I guess I would have to question her commitment, her desire, her drive, and her motivation.

ASK YOURSELF: Why do you want to write?

Let me leave this section with this little vignette:

A woman went backstage after enjoying a New York Philharmonic concert to tell Leonard Bernstein how much she enjoyed the performance. As a finale, the orchestra played selections from Bernstein's West Side Story.

"Oh, maestro," she said, "I would gladly sacrifice my left arm to be able to write and conduct music like that."

Bernstein smiled graciously and said, "I have sacrificed the greater part of my life."

PUBLISHERS — THE SHORT LIST

1.   The **slush pile** is a long shot.

2.   **Don't get discouraged** by rejection.

THE SUBMISSION
PACKAGE ...

FIRST: **You want to create the impression that you are a professional.**

SECOND: **The submission package is: the query letter, the writer's resume, press clippings, and the expanded synopsis.**

THIRD: **Writers who want to write and sell commercial fiction must be equally adept at both writing and then selling what they have written.**

At this point I am making two assumptions:

1.   You have finished your novel.

2.   You want to sell it.

PITFALL

Interestingly enough, this part of the exercise, submitting the novel, is the point where many aspiring novelists fall apart. Why? Anyone with the courage, dedication, commitment, and drive to plow through 100,000 words of the best story ever told should have no trouble breezing through this phase of the drill.

SELLING YOUR BOOK

Let me reduce this phase of your writing career to the simplest terms: You wrote the darn book and now you want to *sell* it. So, now you have to show it to a professional in the publishing business. Not your mother, not your girlfriend, not your writer's support group – you have to show it to a real, live agent or editor.

A RECOMMENDATION

Let's get past the nerves and misgivings about this whole venture. Start by raising your right hand and making this commitment. "I, _____, am going to put together the most professional submission package humanly possible."
Did you mean it? Good. Let's go to work.

COMPONENTS OF THE SUBMISSION PACKAGE

The key components of a submission package are:
1.   The query letter.
2.   A writer's resume.
3.   Any press clippings you might have related to your writing or your expertise in the field you are writing about.
4.   The expanded synopsis.

1. THE QUERY LETTER
A Query Letter Is:
1. Your business card.
2. Your introduction to either an agent or an editor.

A Query Letter Should:
1. Be written in a no-nonsense business format.
2. Be addressed to a specific agent or a specific editor.
3. Contain an opening sentence that hooks the reader.
4. Include a brief (25-word) synopsis of your novel.
5. State that the novel is complete and available.
6. Give relevant contact information.

First Impressions:
The query is the first impression you make on the people who are going to help or hinder you in getting published. Remember what they say about first impressions? Well, the impression you want to create with your submission package is that you are a four-door, shiny-finish, writing professional. That finely honed query letter is the first thing that agent or editor is going to see in your package full of goodies.

Length and more:
A query letter should be one page. It should be meticulously typed and flawless in every respect. Keep in mind that the purpose of this letter is to pique the interest of an individual who is a charter member of a group that includes some of the world's most skeptical and picky people.

Be Concise:
Obviously, your query letter should be concise. It should contain that very brief synopsis of your novel that you wrote as you labored through that reduction from 250 words to 125

words to 25 words. (You did it, didn't you?) I hope so, because now is the time to haul it out. Now you need it.

PIECE BY PIECE EXAMINATION OF THE QUERY LETTER:

A Query Letter Has a No-nonsense Business Format

If you are the least bit uncertain about what constitutes the format of a good business letter, don't guess. Be certain. Every basic communications textbook contains a section of the appropriate style for formal or business correspondence. If you don't know it, go to the library or find a friend who has a crackerjack secretary. A good secretary can explain what goes where. These little professional touches aren't going to sell your book – all they are going to do is get your letter read. This, of course, is why you are writing a query letter in the first place. If the query letter isn't professional and well written, there is no reason for the agent or editor to assume your novel will be professional or well written either.

Use good, white bond stationery of substantial weight. Your letter will appear even more professional if it is personalized with your name and address. If you already have stationery, fine. Don't use anything that has flowers, kittens, or puppies, is some color other than white, or is perfumed. Remember, this is an "I mean business" letter.

Your Query Letter is Addressed to a Specific Person

Double-check the editor's or agent's name and be certain of the correct spelling. Double-check the agency's and/ or publisher's name. Is it correct? Is it spelled correctly? Is the information current? Is it Mr. or Ms.? Invest in a phone call to the publisher's or agency's switchboard to make certain the info you have is correct before you sit down to type. Get the individual's title right. (These people have worked hard for their titles – respect them.)

148

Make certain you date your letter. If you have to call to check on your submission package's whereabouts at a later date, you can refer to "my letter of April 6." That's more professional than stumbling through something like "I sent the package about a month ago."

If all of this sounds painfully fundamental, consider this: I received an important contract last week that wasn't dated. I also received a notice from the post office informing me of my new address – without the zip code. There are a lot of slipshod, ill-conceived performances going on out there. You don't want your query letter to be one.

The Hook:

Your opening sentence should be your *hook*. Remember, the purpose of any business letter is to intrigue the reader enough to read your next sentence. You can hope for no more than that. Tell the person why you are writing. Don't get cute. Don't let *rigor mortis* set in either.

TOO STIFF.

My novel, A Black River, *is available for your consideration.*

Or: **BETTER.**

The setting of my novel, A Black River, *is the high country of the Sawtooth National Forest.*

Or: **TOO WORDY.**

A Black River *is a novel about a weekend-long adventure that turns murderous in the perilous high country of the Sawtooth National Forest.*

149

See how easy it is to overdo? Of the three hook sentences above, the **second** one is probably the best.

Polish that hook sentence until it grabs the reader.

Once again, the hook sentence should be designed to make certain the agent or editor becomes interested enough to go on to the next phase of your query letter – the brief synopsis or 25-word condensation of your plot.

The Brief Synopsis

The focus of your query letter is that 25-word distillation of your plot. Picture yourself in the local video store, trying to decide what movie to rent. How long does it take? Not long, right? You read the blurb on the back of the box, make your decision, and move on. If you took more than 17 seconds to make your view or no-view decision, you have taken longer than the average amount of time. While you may not think it's fair, that's the reality. Tough, huh? Now you know why your brief synopsis has to be well written and succinct.

MY SYNOPSIS:

Here is the synopsis paragraph I wrote for *Deathscape*. (The book was published under the title, *The Lake*.)

Deathscape is a horror novel set in a coastal resort village. It details the six days leading to a cataclysmic Labor Day disaster.

(The reader needs to know that I wrote what eventually hit the market as *The Lake* without a contract. I did not have an agent at the time and my publisher had changed managing editors. Even though I had written and sold books to the same publisher in the past, it was necessary to sell myself all over

150

again to the new managing editor. Bottom line, he bought it. In fact, he was on the phone with an offer two weeks after I submitted my query letter and expanded synopsis.)

The 25-word "brief synopsis" accomplished what it was supposed to accomplish. It gave the editor the information he needed. It told him the **setting of the story** – a resort area (you can work any number of subplots into an area where there is a lot going on), that it **covered only a six-day period – fast, almost an hour-by-hour pace**, and it **would be a *resort* or quick read**. In other words, people would pick it up when they were on vacation and it would not take a great deal of time to read it. That 25-word synopsis not only helps your editor slot the book, genre wise, but to think about how to market it.

Constructing a synopsis that encapsulates your novel and gives the agent or editor sufficient information and reason to continue reading your query letter takes practice. Don't just whittle it down to 25 words and be satisfied. Polish that gem like it is the last opportunity you're going to have to sell your book.

I have included a copy of an example query letter in a later chapter.

Let's Wrap Up This Query Letter Business

Now comes the conclusion to your query letter. Don't kid yourself, this part of the letter is just as important as the earlier components. You tell the recipient of your letter that the novel is complete and that you will send it immediately upon request. (Caution – don't tell them the novel is done if it isn't.)

You're done. Wrap it up. Sign off. Do not hinder your chances by telling the agent or editor what a great novel you have written. They will judge the merits of your work. Don't

151

simper. Don't beg. Never say anything like, "I hope you like my novel."

One final comment:

Make that closing statement a positive one. "I look forward to hearing from you soon." That lets the agent or editor know you consider your time valuable as well. A statement like that conveys just the right touch of author's bravado.

Got it? Good.

The Rest of the Submission Package

While the query letter is the most important part of your submission package, it is only one part. Now we turn our attention to the other components.

2. THE WRITER'S RESUME

First of all, this is not like an employment resume. It has no predetermined format. It should focus on writing or why you believe you are qualified to write about the subject of your novel. Even if this is your first novel, you have doubtless had some writing experience. What was it? Where? When? I'm not a believer in newspaper clippings, so I think you should find a way to encapsulate this information in a fashion that is both intriguing and informative.

Examples:

1.   I met a writer from Ohio several years ago who wanted to write a spy thriller. He had all the tools — a good story line, a good outline, but no actual writing experience. When it came to this resume business, he was stymied. We kept digging, trying to help him find evidence of writing skills in his background. Nothing.

Finally, I asked the question I should have asked way back at the beginning of our session, "Why do you want to write a spy novel?"

"Well," he said, "I was in the CIA for a number of years and I know a lot about it."

Bingo. That's the only thing he needed on his resume. One year later, when his novel was finished, along with the rest of his submission package, he included a single page, one paragraph, "Author's Background." In that one paragraph he mentioned the fact that he had been employed by the CIA and had more than twenty years of service with that agency. He sold the book.

2.   Another writer, not previously published, this time of westerns, living in New Jersey, had trouble getting an agent's attention. Until, that is, she mentioned the fact that she grew up in Montana and had majored in Early American Western history in college. The agent figured she really would have a feel for the West, asked her to forward her manuscript, and decided to represent her.

3.   On the other side of the coin was a lady at one of my seminars who informed the class that she had been published 137 times over the last three years. Her fellow attendees were dazzled. Then she went on to indicate that she had said as much on a recent writer's resume she had submitted with a short story. When I told her I was impressed, she advised me not to be. "That was 137 church bulletins," she informed me, "but they were published."

Relevancy:

The operative word on this writing resume is *relevant*. If it is irrelevant, don't include it. Do include those items that would be of interest to an agent or editor – prior publication credentials or why you are qualified to write about the subject you have chosen. I have included an example of a writer's resume at the back of this book.

3. THE EXPANDED SYNOPSIS

This, like the resume and query letter, is a document that stands alone. Many will tell you that this is an optional part of the package. I disagree. If you've written a crackerjack query letter that includes your 25-word brief synopsis, and you have the agent's or author's attention, why not include it? If the agent or editor thought enough of your package to take it this far, it just makes sense that this is the time to read your whole synopsis.

How Do You Write an Expanded Synopsis?

Author James V. Smith Jr. once said that writing a synopsis is a great deal like telling a friend about the movie you saw the previous evening.

You:

1. Set the scene.
2. Identify the principal characters.
3. Describe the action and march through the story.
4. If inclined, might even drop in a few lines of dialogue if you feel it adds zip to the story you are telling.

It sounds easy – but it isn't.

And You:
1.   Make the synopsis flow.
2.   Include critical plot points.
3.   Describe tensions and conflicts.

You Must:
This is key: Not be afraid to reveal your climax. No one is going to steal it. If you don't include the climax, your reader is going to think you don't have one. Lots of new writers don't. The suspicion is justified.

PITFALL
Remember, this is just another writing project,
albeit, an important one, where your professionalism,
or lack of it, will really show through.

Everything I have stressed about the other components of your submission package applies here as well. Your expanded synopsis should be as slick and polished as you can make it (read that, pure dynamite).
There is an example of an expanded synopsis in this book, near the end.

4. THE FINAL STEP
All the Components:
1.   Your query letter
2.   Your resume
3.   Clippings (if you choose to do so)
4.   Your expanded synopsis

Put the above in one envelope; include a self-addressed, stamped envelope (SASE); take it to the post office;

make certain you have the proper postage on your return package; and mail it.

A RECOMMENDATION
Mark the date that you mailed it down on
the calendar, because you will be convinced
they have had your package four months when
they have only had it four weeks. Allow for the
fact that mail doesn't always get there as fast as
you hoped it would and that the editor to whom
you addressed the package may be out of the
country or even home having a baby. Despite
convincing arguments and opinions to the contrary,
both editors and agents are human.

5. THE FOLLOW UP
How long do you wait to follow up? It varies.
Rejection slips have a way of thundering back. The flip side is,
if an agent or editor likes your work, you will get a phone call.
Some agents, some editors, take forever. Don't assume that all
agents and editors are good at their jobs. You will soon learn
that there are all levels of competence and performance in the
publishing business, just like every other field of endeavor. One
author I know, a man who does a lot of spec work (without a
contract), says he gives an agent four to six weeks, and a
publisher ten to twelve weeks. Then he follows up.

SOME FINAL THOUGHTS ON THE WRITING BUSINESS
This is a tough business. If you are good enough and
tenacious enough, you will make it. But it requires an
investment of both **time and learning** how to do it.

Looking back, that first **writer's workshop** I attended was **one of the best investments I could have made** in my writing career at the time. Those three days on the campus of Ball State University were an emotional roller coaster. One moment I was listening to Clive Cussler tell how he researched his best-selling *Raise the Titanic*, and the next I was talking to struggling newcomers to the writing world – people just like me.

Most of us, I suspect, were guilty of spending too much time wondering about how we were going to sell a novel that we hadn't as yet written. But the fact is that writers who want to write and sell commercial fiction must be **equally adept at both writing and then selling** what they have written. At least that is true of your first novel and maybe even some of those that follow.

Most of you realize that the **odds are against you.** But they are better than winning the lottery or becoming a golfer on the PGA circuit.

A RECOMMENDATION
Do yourself a favor. Prepare to win. Be professional. Double-check everything. Polish, edit, and revise. Taking those few simple steps—admittedly a great deal of work—will help you beat those long odds.

Now, go write your novel.

THE SUBMISSION PACKAGE — THE SHORT LIST

1.   **Make sure you include all the components** in your submission package:
    a.   **The query letter.**
    b.   **A writer's resume**.
    c.   **Press clippings.**
    d.   **The expanded synopsis.**

2.   Write a **concise query letter.**

3.   Make sure you have a **succinct 25 word synopsis** in your letter.

4.   Create an impression that **you are a professional**.

5.   **Double-check everything. Polish, edit and revise.** Taking those few simple steps – admittedly a great deal of work – will help you beat those long odds.

17

FINAL THOUGHTS ...

FIRST: **Talk to other writers.**

SECOND: **Attend writer's workshops.**

THIRD: **Believe in yourself.**

FOURTH: **Be professional.**

FIFTH: **When you become an *author*, help someone else realize his or her dream.**

     In the previous sixteen chapters, I have tried to enumerate and elaborate on many of the **Pitfalls** facing a beginning novelist. As someone once put it, *"The road to glory is paved with hell"* (or words to that effect). When I wrote my first two novels – the ones that no one has ever read — I was just a neophyte in this world of writing. I must have read a dozen books that I hoped would help me understand the nuts and bolts of writing long fiction with a commercial potential.
     Looking back, I didn't learn much from that effort.

I learned by:
1.   Doing,
2.   Talking to other writers,
3.   Attending workshops,
4.   And doing a whole lot of writing.

I attended writer's conferences where:
1.   Listening to Clive Cussler helped.
2.   Hanging on every word Rod Serling said helped.
3.   Heavy doses of the master, John D. MacDonald, taught me some of the finer points of the craft.

All of this took time, and patience, and a great deal of sacrifice.

Visualization:
I'm a believer in visualizing. From the beginning I:
1.   Acted like an author.
2.   Worked like an author.
3.   Thought like an author.

Believe in Yourself:
I always believed I would make it – that I would see my books on the shelves of bookstores with my name in big, bold letters.
It happened.

Every mentor I've ever had insisted on two things:
1.   Be professional.
2.   And, when you do get published, help others learn the ropes.

Helping Others:

     That's why, after plowing my way through, revising, and rewriting my first book on writing, I decided I could carry some of my advice, hints, and tips a bit farther. How? By actually showing examples.

     Along with each example, I have tried to give a little background to explain why I did what I did. Hopefully, these examples will help you better understand some of the material discussed earlier in the handbook.

Now, my charge to you, when you hit your stride as an author: Help someone else realize his or her dream.

FINAL THOUGHTS —
THE SHORT LIST

1. Learn by doing, talking **to other writers,** attending **workshops, and most importantly,** writing **a lot.**

2. **Visualize success** by acting, working and thinking like an author.

3. **Be professional** and, when you get published, **help others**.

18

EXAMPLES: SHOWING, NOT TELLING ...

FIRST: **Whatever you do, outline your story before you begin.**

SECOND: **There are other ways of writing an outline.**

THIRD: **An outline gives you a map of where you're going, and it serves as a reminder of what you need to cover in order to keep the reader up to date.**

THE REASON FOR EXAMPLES:

People who had just sat through one of my day-long seminars on the novel, approached me at its completion and inquired whether I had examples of some of the writing aids I had discussed.

"It's all right for you to describe it," one young woman said, "but I'd sure like to see what one looks like."

"We'd like to see one of yours," another suggested.

After that, I began passing out examples when I came to that point in my presentation. That seemed to quench aspiring

163

writers' thirst for more concrete guides as they worked their way through the maze of their first novel. So, the next few chapters are examples of outlining, query letters, a writer's resume, an expanded synopsis, along with a chapter on good stuff a writer should know.

EXAMPLE: OUTLINE

MY EXPERIENCE: *The Gehenna Effect ...*
     The following outline is for a book titled *The Gehenna Effect*, a techno-thriller that I am currently developing.
     The evolution of this particular story began early in 1997 in a series of telephone conversations with my agent.
     "Sounds confusing without something in front of me," he said, "send me a copy of your outline."
     Which is exactly what I did. Two weeks later, with the story outline in front of him, my agent called the editor. They discussed the story line, the editor advised my agent to make certain I had plenty of "current weapon's technology" in it, and they negotiated the rest (delivery date, advance, royalty percentage, etc.).
     As you will see as you read this, there is plenty of room for me to maneuver even after I've begun to write. The basic story line is there. The editor knows what to expect and begins to think about how and when the book will be slotted. As for me, I can add dimension and detail, take out things that don't work, develop subplots within the overall story line, and, along the way, have tons of fun "showing folks" my story. I am not, as many beginning novelists fear when they first outline the story and put it on paper, hemmed in.
     True, you may not have the advantage of discussing

your proposed story with someone in the publishing business when you sit down to write your first novel, but this example outline worked. Both my editor and agent were convinced I had a solid story to tell.

As you study this example outline, make note of what I have covered.

Situation:	Evidence of massive genocide
Location:	Turkish/Iraqi border
Protagonist:	Commander T.C. (Toby) Bogner
Mission:	Stop genocide/defuse threat of attack
How:	Destroy the facility that produces the toxic agent (you will notice I did not say how I would do this at this point, but I know it has to be a big bang climax).
Time:	Urgent, there is a worldwide bio-nuclear threat.
Urgency:	After carrying the outline development this far, I realize that the success of this story will hinge on the pace that the story is written. It will have to be a bang-bang pace, creating the sense of urgency at the outset – and continually accelerating as the story unfolds.

True, there are other ways of writing an outline. This particular style is what works for me. If you discover something that works better for you, by all means use it. But, whatever you do, outline your story before you begin.

At any rate, here is the outline that I started with when I began work on *The Gehenna Effect*.

165

OUTLINE: THE GEHENNA EFFECT
(R. Karl Largent,12/07/97)

Orbiting Navstar satellites (<u>Navigation System utilizing Time and Ranging</u>) discover, using low orbit vehicles containing telescopes and cameras, disturbing anomalies in the hilly regions along the Turkish-Iraqi border. Over a two-week period, they obtain photographs of several areas where there is no longer any evidence of life forms that are known to exist in that area. This, coupled with information obtained from operatives inside Syria and Jordan, reveal that they have evidence that nomadic and semi-nomadic tribes have been decimated by an unknown illness. In many cases, they are told, even the tribes' herds of cattle, horses, and sheep have been wiped out.

Discrete inquiries are made by the United Nations through Iraq's former ally, Russia, as to what may have contributed to this disaster. Despite what has been learned through the satellite photos, leaders of Iraqi Revolutionary Command Council (RCC) in Baghdad insist there is no problem.

Concurrent with the photos taken of the Iraqi situation, the CIA uncovers an American spy, a chemist, who has been selling top-secret information to Iraq. Included in that information is the formula for HyT-a, a re-formulated and decidedly more deadly version of the old WWI mustard gas that the Iraqi have code named "<u>Gehenna</u>," the Arab word for torment. It is based on a formulation of hyscyamine and icotinix and uses ancine as the base. The formula was developed and stolen from a Nevada test facility where it was *being developed as a 21ˢᵗ century bio-weapon alternative that could be distributed on U.S. long-range nuclear warhead missiles.*

At the time all of this is happening, the Pentagon notes that Iraq is again saber-rattling. The U.S., knowing that Iraq now possesses the necessary missile hardware to deliver such a weapons system, fears that the RCC is about to launch another attack that this time may extend beyond its Arab neighbors. The Americans decide to take action and intervene before such an attack can be launched.

A plan is devised. The U.S. will send a team consisting of their top Internal Security Agency (ISA) trouble shooter, Commander T.C. Bogner (protagonist developed for the Red series), and a young Special Forces explosives expert, Lieutenant Booker Jones, along with two Turkish commandos to destroy the Iraqi facility where the HyT-a is being produced. The mission is designed as a "hit and run" clandestine operation, to be accomplished in one night. The plan is to have the four men taken in by helicopter, dropped off, given ten hours to accomplish their mission and then picked up so that they can escape back into friendly territory inside Saudi Arabia.

The plan, however, goes awry when the low-flying Hughes AH-64 helicopter crashes while carrying the foursome to the mission site inside Iraq. What was conceived as a mission that would take less than twenty-four hours now becomes a three-day ordeal. The two Turkish commandos who are accompanying Bogner and Jones en route to the HyT-a facility are killed along with the crew of the helicopter when it crashes after crossing over the border into Iraq.

The two Americans (Bogner and Jones) are slightly

167

injured but caught in unfamiliar territory. They are discovered by, and eventually win over, two Kurdish nationalists: a young woman and her brother (possible sexual tension element introduced). The Kurds, after learning what the Americans are trying to do, are willing to help them because of their continuing hatred for the Iraqis. (This animosity was developed during the internal war when Iraqi Kurds sided with Iran in the Iraq-Iran war. The young Kurd couple's father was tortured and killed in that war while fighting against the "hated Iraqi RCCs.") When the Americans explain the nature of their mission, the Kurds agree to help them.

By this time, Iraqi patrols have discovered the downed helicopter and are searching the area for survivors. In a series of narrow escapes, the foursome (Bogner, Jones, and the two young Kurds) repeatedly manage to elude the Iraqi search teams. Finally, they reach the secret plant that manufactures the HyT-a. It is situated in the foothills near the tiny village of Ash-Shabakah near the Iraq-Turkish border. They succeed in destroying the facility, but only after the young lieutenant (Jones) and the Kurd woman's brother lose their lives in the final showdown.

Bogner and the attractive young Kurd woman, with Iraqi patrols in hot pursuit, escape back across the border into Turkey. Mission accomplished.

See how simple your story outline can be? Just spell out your story.

Now you have your plot fairly well thought out. Now you take your story apart chapter by chapter.

EXAMPLE: CHAPTER OUTLINE

Thinking in Blocks:

One of the things I have learned to do is think in blocks – chapters, if you will, although I have learned the block may actually turn out to be more than one chapter in the finished work.

Remember the sequence of a novel described in Chapter Eight? This is your *commencement* – your beginning – the kick off. As a novelist, you are trying to accomplish a great many things in this first chapter. You want to establish a sense of the magnitude of the problem your protagonist is about to confront. You want to create a sense of time and place, bring your protagonist into the picture, put that protagonist in a setting that your reader can identify with, and establish a pace (in this case, a very real sense of urgency).

This is the way I sketched out the first block of *The Gehenna Effect*. Note: I will continue to do this, making certain I have each block pretty well thought out before I start it. I work my way through the story this way. Again, this does not freeze me in concrete; it does give me a good map of where I'm going, and it serves as a reminder of what I need to cover in order to keep the reader up to date.

I used to do this on cards, but I have since learned that it is even more convenient to put it in the computer as I go.

THE GEHENNA EFFECT:

BLOCK 1

Scene: *A young officer at the Strategic Assessment Center in the Pentagon receives a routine call from Nellis Air Force Base in Nevada with a code blue-green advisory. The caller describes anomalies discovered in recent satellite photos of a hilly section along the Turkish and Iraqi border. The officer verifies and relays the information to his superior. They discuss what it could be and, since it is a very thinly populated area, write it off as unexplained local phenomena. (Establish date and time line) Four to five pages.*

Scene: A Turkish border patrol guard (desolate area) is conducting his routine morning patrol. He finds the remains of a young Kurd. The corpse is blistered, bloated, and covered with what appear to be burns. This is the third similar incident in the last two weeks, all in the same vicinity. He is aware Kurds have been and continue to flee across the border to find sanctuary in Turkey. He kicks some sand over the body, partially buries it, and proceeds with his patrol. Later that day he reports the incident to his superiors. Four to five pages.

Scene: A Kurd herdsman returns to his village and finds the inhabitants of the entire village dead – bodies are blistered, bloated and covered with what appear to be burns. He finds the bodies of his wife and children. There is no evidence of a struggle. He buries them. Four to five pages.

Scene: (Vault ahead three weeks in time) An old friend of Clancy Packer, ISA chief, calls him. The man is a former college roommate, now a delegate for a group investigating violations of human rights. They have dinner (include Sara) and he describes what he has seen in a Kurd village on the Turkish-Iraqi border. Four to five pages.

Scene: *Introduce Bogner (protagonist). Bogner is returning from a conference in Hawaii. He is not currently on assignment. He and Robert Miller (see* Red Tide *for intro) stop in at a local pub for a drink, discuss matters (this will give readers partial background on Bogner); and Miller brings Bogner up to speed on agency matters. This is where Bogner learns of the situation along the Turkish-Iraqi border for the first time. Miller informs Bogner that the area where the bodies were found is reasonably close to the site where U.S. spy satellites have taken photos that reveal an Iraqi plant has been built. Miller also tells him that the Iraqi government claims the facility was erected to make pharmaceuticals. Four to five pages.*

The above is the first chapter outline of *The Gehenna Effect* as I originally laid it out. The reader should know that there were actually two more scenes which I did not think it necessary to elaborate on in this example.

Again let me say that just as there is with the overall outline of the plot, there are several ways to do a chapter-by-chapter outline as well. This is the way I do it. It keeps me on track and it also keeps me from straying too far from what the reader needs to know at any given point in the development of the story. Even more important, I'm less likely to forget some critical element that would later result in the necessity to rewrite the entire chapter.

I go through this routine before I start every chapter and I keep it close by the computer when I'm working on that particular phase of the story.

171

EXAMPLES: SHOWING, NOT TELLING... THE SHORT LIST

1.   **Learn to outline**; it'll make your life **easier**.

2.   **Learn to think in blocks.** Blocks are simpler to build with.

EXAMPLE: A QUERY LETTER ...

FIRST: **This letter is your business introduction – an agent's or publisher's first impression of you and your work.**

SECOND: **Be brief, concise and professional.**

I checked with several author friends of mine before I decided to suggest the following format for a query letter. Each agreed that if an unpublished author was sending a query letter to a specific editor at a publisher or one particular agent in a large literary agency, this format would be appropriate.

The letter, of course, would be meticulously typed on no-nonsense, personalized, or business-like stationery. It would be centered in the middle of the page, and you would make certain to sign it.

Remember, this letter is your business introduction. In many ways it is like a business card. This letter is that agent's or editor's first impression of you and your work. You know what they say about first impressions.

Your Name
Your Address
Your City, State and Zip
Your Telephone Number

Date

Person's name
Title
Agency or Publisher's Company
Street Address
City, State, Zip

Dear Mr. (Ms.) Specific Name: (1)

My recently completed horror novel, *Deathscape*, focuses on a large scale ecological disaster. (2)

Deathscape takes place in a coastal resort village and details the events leading up to a cataclysmic Labor Day disaster in which thousands perish. (3)

An expanded synopsis of the manuscript is attached. The complete manuscript of *Deathscape* is available upon request. (4)

Thank you for your time and consideration. I look forward to your prompt response. (5)

Signature

WHY DOES THIS LETTER WORK

To start with it is brief, concise and professional, the way a business letter should be.

(1) The letter is directed to a specific individual.

(2) The hook sentence is there, getting the reader into the letter.

(3) Your carefully constructed 25-word synopsis tells the agent or editor what your novel is about.

(4) Your reader knows the expanded synopsis is attached and that the finished manuscript is available.

(5) A "thank you" is nothing more than common courtesy. Plus, you have included a gentle but professional prod that shows you expect a prompt response.

BUSINESS STATIONERY

One colleague of mine strongly recommended investing in personalized *business* stationery for your query letter. It is easy and inexpensive to obtain. Trot down to your local quick print or office supply store, ask them to design and then run some off for you.

While you're at it, have some business cards printed that

compliment the stationery. It'll make you look all the more professional.

Is all the extra effort worth it? Absolutely. By now you realize that, if you are trying to break into the writing game, you are going to need every advantage you can conjure up.

EXAMPLE: A BEGINNING NOVELIST'S RESUME ...

FIRST: Design a brief one or two-paragraph resume to explain why you are qualified to write about the subject of your novel.

SECOND: A resume is intended to represent you in the best possible light.

The following resume is presented only to give the aspiring novelist with minimum writing credentials an idea of how he or she might go about it. Obviously, if you are an experienced writer with a wide variety of credits in the field, you already have a resume.

All you are trying to accomplish in this brief one or two-paragraph resume is to explain why you believe you have the qualifications to write about the subject you tackle in your novel.

A RECOMMENDATION
What are your qualifications?
Think about it. Make a list.

QUALIFICATIONS: EXAMPLE ...

My doctor is an aspiring novelist and a very good writer. Since most of us tend to write about – at least in the first novel – what we know best, he is working on a novel with a strong medical theme. His resume would logically include the fact that he is a doctor and the assumption will be that he can write about the kind of events that take place in his novel.

LENGTH:

How long should this resume be? Who knows? But it should be **brief**. This is not a prelude to a romantic liaison. This is about your qualifications or familiarity with the subject of your novel.

ABOUT THE AUTHOR:

One or two carefully constructed paragraphs (on a separate page from everything else in your submission package) under the title, "About the Author" (or something similar), detailing your familiarity with the kind of events that take place in your novel should do it. Like your query letter, it should be centered on the page and include a few, if you wish, copies of any press clippings or letters that support your claims.

In the case of my doctor, a list of degrees couldn't hurt either.

1. Don't boast.
2. On the other hand, a resume is no place for "aw, shucks" modesty.

178

THE BOTTOM LINE:
If the editor is not intrigued by what he or she reads in your query letter and synopsis, no amount of credential presenting will change their mind.
RESUME FOR THE NOVICE WRITER

ABOUT THE AUTHOR: AN EXAMPLE...
Prior to authoring my spy novel, The Informer, *I spent 20 years in the United States Diplomatic Service. Five of those years were spent as aide to Ambassador Brant at the American Embassy in Jakarta. During that tour of duty, I had the opportunity to witness, first hand, the attempted coup by General Bojoni Sarawak.*

The Informer is a fictionalized story of Sarawak's coup attempt, resituated in modern day Java, but based on my notes, ordeals, observations, personal diary, and recollections of Sarawak's plan to overthrow the Maylay government.

Well, what do you think? It won't win any prizes for literature, but...

1. It is concise.
2. It does tell the reader what you want the reader to know.

PERMISSION TO NOT INCLUDE A RESUME:
If you have thought about this resume matter long and hard and can come up with nothing that ties you to the kind of novel you have written, forget the resume. I have never heard

an agent or editor say they took on a specific writer solely because of a resume. The acid test in the publishing game is this: **If they like your story, it doesn't matter how you developed your expertise.**

THE PURPOSE OF THE WRITER'S RESUME

Whether you are an old pro or a raw beginner, a resume is to represent yourself in the best possible light. Advice: If it doesn't sound professional and doesn't present you in a favorable light, don't do it. If it does present you in a favorable light, by all means, include that resume in your submission package.

EXAMPLE: THE
EXPANDED SYNOPSIS ...

FIRST: **Check with your editor or agent for their preference: Synopsis or chapters.**

SECOND: **An expanded synopsis will flesh out key characters and elaborate a bit on the subplots in telling about your book.**

Haul out that outline, the one that you didn't want to write and see how it compares with the final product.

It's probably safe to say that you made some changes along the way. Okay, great. You wouldn't have strayed from the original if you hadn't had a better idea or developed a more dynamite climax, would you?

A RECOMMENDATION
Now, you update your outline, flesh out a couple of the key characters, elaborate a bit on the subplots, and in three, four, or five double-spaced, keyboarded pages, tell them about your book. Don't forget to include that terrific ending.

Now you write your synopsis.

EXAMPLE: *Red Skies ...*

PREMISE

The story deals with a radical faction of the PRC (Peoples' Republic of China), known as the Fifth Academy (5A). 5A does not want the USA and Russia to continue to heal their philosophical, diplomatic and political differences. Reason: If that happens, the PRC will be the sole remaining stronghold of Communism in the world.

BACKGROUND

*It is early August and there is a heat wave in Indianapolis. It is the eve of the **Brickyard 400**, the newest crown jewel in NASCAR's season long racing series. On a sultry, Saturday afternoon, over 300,000 people will gather in the famed Speedway to watch the race. Freeways are crowded, the city is jammed with racing fans, hotels and tourist attractions are taxed to capacity. People are edgy, nervous – attributed to the relentless heat wave, but also because 5A terrorists have warned that what happened in Great Britain and Mexico "could happen in the USA as well."*

... The Royal Opera House in London was bombed during a performance of Verdi's Aida, 267 died, 742 injured (June 16, birthday of the Queen). The Queen and her entourage left the opera house just moments before the explosion.
...An off-shore oil rig is blown up off the coast of Mexico, kills

187, injures another 231 on May 5 (Cinco de Mayo). The Mexican President escapes, leaving the rig just moments before the explosion.

*Now Americans fear an attack. But we don't know where; we don't know when. We only know that we have been warned. The American President is planning to attend (note thread of continuity – heads of state) the **Brickyard 400** and the ISA is monitoring activity of known 5A sympathizers. (They are in the Indianapolis area.)*

PROLOGUE

*The prologue is the terrorist attack at the Indianapolis Motor Speedway during the **Brickyard 400**. Seventeen hundred people are killed, thousands are injured. (Prologue is lengthy; could be a first chapter by noting time delineation.)*

THE STORY

Against this backdrop, the ISA (Internal Security Agency) is informed that an important Eastern Bloc aircraft designer, Milo Schubatis, is coming to the United States for an international conference. Schubatis is the man behind the Su-39 (comparable to our F-117). This is happening simultaneous with the defection of a Russian pilot with one of the two prototype Su-39 (NATO designation: Covert). He has defected to 5A. The Americans suspect this, but are unable to confirm it.

At the same time, ISA is alerted to a possible abduction plot of

Schubatis by the 5A, located on the island of Hainan in south China.

ISA Chief, Clancy Packer, assigns T.C. Bogner responsibility for Schubatis' safety while he is in this country. On the way from the airport, the terrorists strike. The terrorists abduct Schubatis and leave the corpse of a badly burned Schubatis look-alike in his place. The bogus Schubatis' real identity is discovered during the ensuing autopsy.

5A manages to get the real Schubatis out of the country. Simultaneous with the discovery that Schubatis is still alive, American agents on Hainan report that they have discovered the whereabouts of the missing Su-39. Now it is clear what 5A is doing. They have the plane and the designer of the plane. They are now in a power position. When the ISA learns this, Bogner is dispatched to Hainan to recover Schubatis and, if possible, fly the Su-39 out of the 5A compound. If he cannot recover the Su-39, he has been instructed to destroy it (We learned earlier that the other Su-39 prototype has previously crashed and is destroyed).

Bogner's cover is as a Canadian arms dealer who is interested in doing business with the dissident 5A faction of the Red Army. He works with the US agent in Hainan, Shu Li, an attractive, American educated, Chinese national, who has contacts within the 5A compound of Danjia.

Meanwhile, his Chinese captors incarcerate an uncooperative Schubatis, still suffering from injuries in the terrorist attack. The leader of the 5A is Mao Quan, who has political ambitions to take over PRC leadership.

Bogner and Shu Li need help getting into the compound. They elicit the help of an aging Catholic priest who maintains an orphanage not far from the Danjia compound. The priest, with ties to the Chinese Nationalist Government on Taiwan, and with the aid of a former Chinese Nationalist pilot, has reassembled an old WW-II helicopter that is kept hidden and used to transport targets of 5A brutality to a small island off the coast of Hainan and eventual political asylum.

A two-stage plan is devised whereby they can get Schubatis out of the compound and at the same time destroy the Su-39. The mission is accomplished, but Colonel Mao Quan (the central antagonist and commanding officer of the 5A compound) discovers where they have taken Schubatis and orders his troops to recapture Schubatis and destroy the orphanage. The old priest is killed, but Bogner, Schubatis, and the young officer escape. When Quan learns this, he dispatches two Sukhoi Su-27 Flankers to abort Bogner's attempt to fly the helicopter to the small island that offers political asylum. Quan would rather have Schubatis dead than have the Russian live to reveal his plan to take over PRC leadership.

Bogner manages to destroy one of the 5A's pursuing planes, but the helicopter is hit, crashes on the small island, and the remaining Flanker fires missiles at the downed helicopter. From the ground, Bogner manages to destroy the remaining Su-27. They have escaped (only temporarily).

But Quan is not done. He learns how the Americans plan to

*get Schubatis off the island and leads a death squad to finish
the job. There is a final assassination attempt at the docks
where the Americans have made arrangements to pick up
Bogner, Schubatis, and the young Chinese officer. The attempt
fails and Quan flees.*

*The trio boards an old freighter that will take them to Macao
where they will catch a flight back to the states. But Quan has
secretly boarded the freighter (it is now a personal vendetta
and Quan is out of control) where there will be a final
confrontation. Quan kills Schubatis. Bogner kills Quan.*

*As the book ends, Bogner is standing in the airport at Macao.
He is reporting in to Packer. The Su-39 is destroyed and the
man who designed and built it is dead. The mission is both a
success...and a failure.*

That wasn't so difficult was it?

CHECK WITH YOUR EDITOR OR AGENT ABOUT THEIR PREFERENCE

1.   I have author friends who write a 10-or-12 page
        synopsis to include in their submission package.

2.   Others may include one, two, even three chapters of the
        novel (usually the first three).

3.   It all depends on the preference of the editor or agent.

4.   Some agents and editors are trying to evaluate the
        quality of your writing while others are determining

whether or not you have a whole story.

5.   That business-like phone call you made to verify the name of the individual (for spelling purposes) and whether or not they are accepting new writers will tell you what they want you to include in the submission package.

THE COMPLETED PACKAGE

There it is:
Your query letter.
Your writer's resume.
Your expanded synopsis chapters,
and the equally important SASE.

That submission package you anguished over and stewed about is now complete. It wasn't that difficult was it? In fact, I know what you're thinking, *actually it was a piece of cake.*

MY EXPERIENCE: Wasted time ...
Looking back, I can't believe how much time and money I wasted back in the days when I was going about the business of writing my own first novels. I'm convinced I committed every blunder, every clinker, and every mistake possible in the process. Fifteen years later I know better, but think how much easier my path to the bookshelves of bookstores would have been if only I had known what I have

tried to impart in this book to the aspiring novelist.

My hope is that this effort will make your journey to those same bookshelves both smoother and quicker.

GOOD STUFF FYI ...

MORE STUFF A WRITER NEEDS TO KNOW

Don't rely on your computer, word processor, whatever, to be the end-all in helping you construct a sentence that reads just exactly the way you want it to read.

Most software cannot distinguish between *they're, there,* and *their.* Nor can it distinguish between a whole host of other homonyms (words with the same pronunciation but with a different meaning).

Such computer writing aids as spell check and word search are not foolproof. If you should happen to type the word *infallible* when you intended to write *ineffable* your word processing package wouldn't know the difference – but your editor will.

To conquer these hurdles, there are several books I find invaluable when I'm writing. They are always close at hand:

1.   A good **dictionary** such as ... *Webster's New World Dictionary.*

2.   Buy yourself a copy of ...*The Synonym Finder,* published by Saint Martin's Press.

3. Get yourself a good **visual dictionary** such as Dorling Kindersley's *Ultimate Visual Dictionary.*

4. Equally important as a good dictionary is *The Penguin Spelling Dictionary.*

... and keep them updated.

OTHER STUFF A WRITER NEEDS TO KNOW

During the course of constructing your manuscript, some specific items should be in italics. If your equipment does not provide this capability, underline the following:

Item	Example
Aircraft	*Spirit of Saint Louis*
Books/Novels	*Hunt for Red October*
Dramas	*Streetcar Named Desire*
Films	*Poltergeist*
Magazines	*Newsweek*
Newspapers	*Chicago Tribune*
Operas	*Rigoletto*
Paintings	*The Last Supper*
Periodicals	*Scientific American*
Radio Programs	*The Lone Ranger*
Recordings	*Fever*
Sculpture	*David*
Ships	*Titanic*
Symphony	*Eroica*
Television	*Tonight Show*

Failure to do so may not be enough to get an editor to reject your manuscript, but it's a sign you're not a pro.

190

ON THE SUBJECT OF HAVING SOMEONE READ YOUR MANUSCRIPT

Several years ago at a workshop at Augustana College, I agreed to comment on a few manuscripts. Among the writers was a highly regarded man in a nearby community, wealthy and very successful in a field other than writing. He handed me a manuscript that had already received high praise by several other people, all close to him. I was convinced that he expected me to put some sort of official blessing on the work before he sent it off to some publisher and catapulted his way to fame and fortune in yet another field of endeavor.

The manuscript was terrible. It was poorly arranged, poorly planned, and poorly written. Three strikes, you're out! I read it, and dreaded telling him what I saw, but in a subsequent one-on-one session I told him exactly what I thought. He looked at me with tears in his eyes, "Finally," he said, "someone is being honest with me. I knew it wasn't ready, but no one would or could tell me what was wrong with it or what I needed to do to fix it. Look at the time that has been wasted."

MORAL: You need a *knowledgeable* person to tell you what is wrong with your manuscript while it is still in the construction phase. Anything less may be counter productive.

SOMETHING TO THINK ABOUT

David Collins, noted children's author, once said it was as important for an aspiring author to know why he wanted to write a particular book as it was to know the story he was about
to tell. Weeks later, during one of my writing seminars, I repeated David's statement to my students and asked them why they wanted to write a novel. Most of the responses could have

been anticipated:

> *"I've always wanted to write a book."*
> *"I want to be rich and famous."*
> *"I think I have something to say."*
> *"I want to walk in a bookstore and see my book."*
> *"I think it would be neat to live like an author."*
> *"My husband thinks I would be a good storyteller."*
> *"People tell me I should write a book."*
> *"I love books."*

QUESTION: Know what's wrong with these responses?

ANSWER: These reasons aren't specific enough. They are much too vague to continue to motivate you when you need that drive to keep at it.

Be specific. Stephen King is. He says, "When I sit down to write a book, I have one purpose in mind; to scare the hell out of you." See what I mean? That, my aspiring novelist friend, is a specific reason.

NEED A LITTLE ENCOURAGEMENT?

At a recent writer's conference I happened to overhear a woman, scheduled for a meeting with an agent, say that if the agent didn't like her story, she was through writing. She claimed she had spent three years on her novel, and all she had were six rejections to show for her efforts.

I wonder if she knew that Mark Twain claims to have accumulated over 1, 000 rejections before he made it? Did she know that Harper Lee's *To Kill a Mockingbird*, had to be rewritten 11 times before the publisher bought it? Believe me, Stephen King, Clive Cussler, and a host of other top-selling authors can recite chapter and verse on rejections.

My own first published novel, *Black Death*, was mailed to six different publishers before the seventh bought it.

MORAL: Don't get discouraged. Put those rejections in a file and then have yourself a nice little ritual bonfire when you sign that contract on your first soon-to-be-published novel.

AND FINALLY ... PYBIACASW

Now, I'd like to leave you with the secret to becoming a real for sure author. It is the truth every published writer before you has had to learn. There is no other way to become an author. Write it down. Tape it to your computer.

What does it stand for?

"Plant your butt in a chair and start writing."

Oh ... and one more thing. Good luck. God Speed. And may the Master Author be with you.

Printed in the United States
4817

9 780964 560628